The I Ching: Text and Annotated Translation

Modern Chinese translation by Liu Dajun and Lin Zhongjun
English translation by Fu Youde
Revision by Frank Lauran

Shandong Friendship Publishing House

First Edition 1995
ISBN 7—80551—696—0/B · 5

Published by
Shandong Friendship Publishing House
Shengli Street, Jinan, China
Printed by
Shandong People's Printing House
Distributed by
China International Book Trading Corporation
35 Chegongzhuang Xilu, Beijing 100044, China
P. O. Box 399, Beijing, China

Printed in the People's Republic of China

Translator's Note

I hesitated when I was first asked by an editor of Shandong Friendship Publishing House to translate Professor Liu Dajun and Mr. Lin Zhongjun's collaborative work *The Modern Chinese Translation and Annotations of the Ancient Text of Zhou Yi* into English. My hesitation was partly because of my awareness of the difficulties in translating and partly because of my devotion to a programme of Jewish culture which I have recently undertaken. I accepted the task when I was asked the second time as I had come to understand its great significance. Thus this book was completed two months later.

I slightly changed the title and put the translation before the notes (they are in the reverse order in the Chinese) for the purpose of fitting the common English practice. In the course of the translation I made efforts to correctly understand and explicitly interpret the implications of the original Chinese text. Meanwhile I also revised a little when really necessary. In addition to keeping the Chinese text of *I Ching*, I also added the Chinese pronunciation to almost all Chinese phrases or characters in the notes in order to benefit those who are inclined to read the Chinese text.

I am grateful to Mr. Frank Lauran, an American working at Shandong University now, for his friendly and efficient assistance with my work. I am also much in debt to Ms. Liang

Jisheng, the production editor for her concern with my translation, to Ms. Tan Siqian for her typing the Chinese text of *I Ching* and to my wife Zhong Suzhen for her help in many ways.

Fu Youde
November 4, 1994

Preface

The idea to add notes to the classical text of *I Ching* occured to me in 1970. However, I was not in a position to start till in 1973 because of the shortage of materials and the political climate. The first draft was finished in the winter of 1976. I was not satisfied with it and therefore put it aside.

Shortly after I became a lecturer at Shandong University, I revised and mimeographed the annotations of the first twelve hexagrams, that is, from Hexagram Heaven (Qian) to Hexagram Obstruction(Pi), as a student textbook. It was on this basis that I completed the annotations as well as the revision of the other hexagrams in June, 1984. It was the second draft. While copying the manuscript I found in the *Journal of Cultural Relics*, volume 3 (1984) the transcript of the sixty-four hexagrams of the *I Ching* unearthed in the Han Tombs of Mawangdui and now called the *I Ching on Silk* as well as the following two articles: " A Postscript to the Sixty-four Hexagrams of the *I Ching on Silk* " by Zhang Zhenglang and " The Text of the *I Ching on Silk* " by Yu Haoliang. The unearthing of the silk text was of surprising significance in the academic field in the early 80s because it differs from the existing text not only in the order of the sixty-four hexagrams but also in a number of hexagram names, interpretive words of the hexagrams and their lines. Faced with this early Han Dynasty text, should I ignore it and put the first finished manuscript into print or revise it again using it? I chose the latter with no hesitation. Thus I put the manuscript aside temporarily and turned to careful study of the *I Ching on Silk*. It was not easy because there were no reference books available at that time. Soon after, I was asked to do another work, the collation of *Yu Fan's Annotations of I Ching*, which took me almost two years to complete. Therefore I did not finish the revision of my own annotations and translation using the *I Ching on Silk* as reference until the end of 1987. That was the third draft. Later, with the efficient collaboration of Mr. Lin Zhongjun we finished the final revision. In the course of our cooperative work, some parts of the book were rewritten and added by Mr. Lin and the work was finally completed in his hand. That was the fourth draft.

In short, what the reader will read is not a collection of the previous scholars' annotations but a synthetic product in which the contents of the *I Ching on Silk* is also included.

The book is written for the reader who has difficulties in reading the classical text of the *I Ching*. For this reason, following the standard Chinese " three-character guide " of translation, i. e. faithfulness, expressiveness and elegance, we made efforts to translate the text of the hexagrams and their interpretive lines into modern Chinese, striving to correctly express the meaning of the original text and maintain its style. As we all know, however, to study the *I Ching* in depth is not an easy thing; and to interpret its profound and mysterious implications in modern Chinese is even more difficult. Therefore although we have done our best and completed four drafts in the course of our work, we are still rather unsatisfied with it and regret that we have not been able to better meet the need of our readers.

Thanks to Shandong Friendship Publishing House this book can be published. We are particularly in debt to its production editor who visited me five times and showed her whole-hearted enthusiasm for our work. We are also grateful to Ms. Cong Ying for her labour in sorting out data and transcribing the manuscript of this book.

Liu Dajun
May 1989

Contents

Part One

Hexagram 1 Heaven (Qian)
Hexagram 2 Earth (Kun)
Hexagram 3 Difficulty (Zhun)
Hexagram 4 Immaturity (Meng)
Hexagram 5 Waiting (Xu)
Hexagram 6 Contention (Song)
Hexagram 7 Army (Shi)
Hexagram 8 Trust (Bi)
Hexagram 9 Little Increment (Xiao Xu)
Hexagram 10 Treading (Lu)
Hexagram 11 Peace (Tai)
Hexagram 12 Obstruction (Pi)
Hexagram 13 Fellowship (Tong Ren)
Hexagram 14 Great Possession (Da You)
Hexagram 15 Modesty (Qian)
Hexagram 16 Enjoyment (Yu)
Hexagram 17 Following (Sui)
Hexagram 18 Decay (Gu)
Hexagram 19 Looking Down (Lin)
Hexagram 20 Observing (Guan)
Hexagram 21 Biting (Shi He)
Hexagram 22 Adornment (Bi)

Hexagram 23 Stripping Away (Bao)

Hexagram 24 Return (Fu)

Hexagram 25 The Unexpected (Wu Wang)

Hexagram 26 Great Increment (Da Xu)

Hexagram 27 Nourishment (Yi)

Hexagram 28 Great Fault (Da Guo)

Hexagram 29 Watery Danger (Kan)

Hexagram 30 Fire (Li)

Part Two

Hexagram 31 Sensation (Xian)

Hexagram 32 Constancy (Heng)

Hexagram 33 Little Pig (Dun)

Hexagram 34 Great Power (Da Zhuang)

Hexagram 35 Advance (Jin)

Hexagram 36 Darkness (Ming Yi)

Hexagram 37 Family (Jia Ren)

Hexagram 38 Conflict (Kui)

Hexagram 39 Trouble (Jian)

Hexagram 40 Release (Jie)

Hexagram 41 Loss (Sun)

Hexagram 42 Gain (Yi)

Hexagram 43 Resolution (Guai)

Hexagram 44 Meeting (Gou)

Hexagram 45 Assembling (Cui)

Hexagram 46 Ascending (Sheng)

Hexagram 47 Adversity (Kun)

Hexagram 48 The Well (Jing)

Hexagram 49 Revolution (Ge)

Hexagram 50 The Cauldron (Ding)

Hexagram 51 Thunder (Zhen)

Hexagram 52 Keeping Still (Gen)

Hexagram 53 Gradual Progress (Jian)

Hexagram 54 Marrying Maiden (Gui Mei)

Hexagram 55 Abundance (Feng)

Hexagram 56 The Traveller (Lu)

Hexagram 57 Calculation (Xun)

Hexagram 58 Joy (Dui)

Hexagram 59 Flowing (Huan)

Hexagram 60 Restraint (Jie)

Hexagram 61 Inner Faithfulness (Zhong Fu)

Hexagram 62 Small Fault (Xiao Guo)

Hexagram 63 Fulfilment (Ji Ji)

Hexagram 64 Unfulfilment (Wei Ji)

Part One

Hexagram 1
乾(Qian) Heaven

The Chinese text:

乾¹：元亨，利贞²。
初九³：潜龙勿用⁴。
九二：见龙在田⁵，利见大人⁶。
九三：君子终日乾乾⁷，夕惕若厉⁸，无咎⁹。
九四：或跃在渊¹⁰，无咎。
九五：飞龙在天，利见大人。
上九：亢龙有悔¹¹。
用九¹²：见群龙，无首吉¹³。

Translation:

Heaven: It is favourable for one to consult one's fortune when one has attained great success at the beginning.

Nine at the bottom line: The dragon is hidden. Do not take rash action.

Nine at the second line: The dragon appears in the fields. It is advantageous to see a great man.

Nine at the third line: The superior man works diligently and steadily in the day time and keeps alert in the evening as if he were in danger. No harm.

Nine at the fourth line: The dragon is about to leap but not yet in motion. No disaster.

Nine at the fifth line: The dragon is flying in the sky. It is auspicious to meet a great man.

Nine at the top line: The dragon flying at extreme height leads to regret.

All six yang lines: A group of dragons appear without a leader. Good fortune.

Notes:

1. 乾(qian): it is written as 键(jian) in the *I Ching on Silk*, (one of the most valuable transcripts of the *I Ching*, copied by hand on silk cloth during the Han Dynasty), indicating firmness and obduracy. In the ancient text of the *I Ching*, each hexagram is composed of six horizontal lines among which some are undivided ——, and some are divided — —, being called respectively yang lines and yin lines. This hexagram consists of six yang lines and symbolizes heaven.

2. 元亨,利贞(yuan heng li zhen): interpretive words of the hexagram Qian. 元(yuan): beginning or start. 亨(heng): unobstructed or succesful. 利(li): advantageous or favourable. 贞(zhen): steadfast and faithful or divination; here meaning the latter.

3. 初九(chu jiu): the first line of each hexagram is pronounced *chu*, meaning the first. All undivided lines, that is, yang lines, of the sixty four hexagrams of the *I Ching* are named nine (*jiu*) and all divided lines, yin lines, six (*liu*). Therefore, from the bottom to the top, the six undivided lines of this hexagram are respectively called the first nine, the second nine, the third nine, the forth nine, the fifth nine and the top nine. Similarly, all the divided lines of next hexagram *Qun*, the earth, are called the first six, the second six, the third six, the forth six, the fifth six and the top six.

4. 潜龙勿用(qian long wu yong): the dragon is in concealment. Do not take rash action. 潜(qian): hidden or concealed. 龙(long): dragon. In ancient China it designated auspiciousness and was divinized as the god of spring and rain, and the ancient Chinese offered a sacrifice to the

dragon for rain. Regarding the archtype of the dragon, some scholars take it as boa, snake, lizard or crocodile and the like. Others consider it a representation of the rain-bow. The dragon is chosen in the *I Ching* to stand for vital breath and a superior man.

5. 见龙在田 (xian long zai tian): the dragon appears in the fields. 见 (xian): emerge or appear.

6. 利见大人 (li jian da ren): favourable to see the great man. 大人 (da ren): a person in a powerful position, a great man.

7. 乾乾 (qian qian): work diligently and steadily.

8. 夕惕若厉 (xi ti ruo li): to be alert in the evening as if one were in danger. 厉 (li): danger. 惕 (ti): be alert.

9. 无咎 (wu jiu): no harm, no disaster or good fortune.

10. 或跃在渊 (huo yue zai yuan): the dragon in the abyss is about to leap but is not yet in action. 或 (huo) may be interpreted as 惑 (huo), meaning someone, some person; or perplexity and hesitation; here it means the latter.

11. 亢龙有悔 (kang long you hui): the dragon flying at extreme height results in regret. 亢 (kang): very high.

12. 用九 (yong jiu) is written as 迵九 (tong jiu) in the *I Ching on Silk*, meaning all the lines of the hexagram Qian are nine or yang lines.

13. 无首吉 (wu shou ji): no leader of the group of dragons indicates good fortune.

Hexagram 2
坤 (Kun): Earth

The Chinese text:

坤[1]：元亨，利牝马之贞[2]。君子有攸往[3]，先迷后得主[4]。利西南得朋，东北丧朋[5]。安贞吉[6]。

初六：履霜，坚冰至[7]。

六二：直方大[8]，不习无不利[9]。

六三：含章可贞[10]，或从王事，无成有终[11]。

六四：括囊，无咎、无誉[12]。

六五：黄裳元吉[13]。

上六：龙战于野，其血玄黄[14]。

用六：利永贞[15]。

Translation：

Earth：Have a great success at the beginning. This divination is auspicious to the rider of a mare. A superior man who has started his trip for a destination will go astray at first and later meet his patron. Going south-west, he will gain friends but the friends may be lost if he goes north-east. Goodfortune follows the observance of the steadfast faithfulness.

Six at the bottom line：Treading on frost one should be aware that hard ice is coming in the near future.

Six at the second line：Stretching far off into the distance and out of one's sight whether one goes straight forward or turns to the side. Do not practise anything and everything will be advantageous.

Six at the third line：A person with virtue is able to observe the principle of steadfast faithfulness.

Six at the fourth line：Tying a sack closed results in neither disaster nor glory.

Six at the fifth line：Wearing yellow pants from the start brings good fortune.

Six at the top line：The dragons fighting in the field shed blood which, mixed with the earth, appears black and yellow.

All six yin lines：A good result comes if one always keeps the principle of steadfast faithfulness.

Notes:

1. 坤(kun): all lines of this hexagram are yin lines and therefore are read " six. " In the ancient text of *I Ching* it was written as 巛 and in the *I Ching on Silk*, it was represented by 川(chuan), meaning rivers. It symbolizes the earth here, indicating a mild and obedient personality.
2. 利牝马之贞(li pin ma zhi zhen): before distant travel, horse riders would consult the omens of their trips. This hexagram is favourable to the rider of a mare. 牝马(pin ma): mare. 贞(zhen): divination or fortune-telling.
3. 有攸往(you you wang): have started one's trip for a destination. 攸(you): have a destination.
4. 先迷后得主(xian mi hou de zhu): go astray at first and later meet a patron.
5. 利西南得朋,东北丧朋(li xi nan de peng, dong bei sang peng): one may gain friends if one travels south-west; the friends may be lost if one goes north-east. 朋(peng): friend. It also signifies a money unit made of shell in ancient China.
6. 安贞吉(an zhen ji): good fortune if one follows the principle of steadfast faithfulness. 贞 (zhen): the principle of steadfast faithfulness.
7. 履霜,坚冰至(lu shuang, jian bing zhi): frost underfoot indicates the coming of hard ice in the near future. 履(lu): tread, walk on.
8. 直方大(zhi fang da): stretch far off into the distance and out of one's sight whether one goes straight forward or turns to the side. 直(zhi): go straight forward. 方(fang): turn to the side.
9. 不习无不利(bu xi wu bu li): do not practise anything and nothing is disadvantageous. 不习(bu xi): do not practise.
10. 含章可贞(han zhang ke zhen): a virtuous person is able to follow the principle of steadfast faithfulness. 章(zhang): morality or virtue.

11. 或从王事，无成有终(huo cong wang shi, wu cheng you zhong)：should one serve the king, one cannot make great achievement but will end well. 终(zhong)：end well or have good result in the end.

12. 括囊，无咎，无誉(kuo nang, wu jiu, wu yu)：tying a sack closed results in neither disaster nor glory.

13. 黄裳元吉(huang shang yuan ji)：wearing yellow skirts or pants is auspicious from the start. 黄（huang）：yellow. The colour was thought of as a sign of good luck in the Zhou Dynasty. 裳(shang)：pants or skirts, excluding jacket in ancient China.

14. 其血玄黄(qi xue xuan huang)：the blood of the dragon shed on the earth appeared black and yellow. 玄(xuan)：deep black.

15. 利永贞(li yong zhen)：favourable to always keep the principle of steadfast faithfulness.

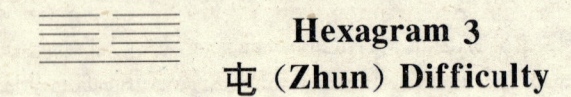

Hexagram 3
屯（Zhun）Difficulty

The Chinese text：

屯[1]：元亨，利贞。勿用有攸往[2]，利建侯[3]。
初九：磐桓[4]，利居贞[5]，利建侯。
六二：屯如邅如[6]，乘马班如[7]。匪寇婚媾[8]，女子贞，不字[9]，十年乃字。
六三：即鹿无虞[10]，惟入于林中。君子几，不如舍[11]，往吝[12]。
六四：乘马班如，求婚媾，往，吉无不利。
九五：屯其膏[13]。小，贞吉；大，贞凶[14]。
上六：乘马班如，泣血涟如[15]。

Translation：

Difficulty：It is favourable for one to consult one's fortune if one has

8

great success at the beginning. Do not travel. To grant the title of duke is advantageous.

Nine at the bottom line: Pace up and down without making progress. It is favourable to observe the principle of steadfast faithfulness and to grant the title of duke.

Six at the second line: One is in a difficult situation and can only go around in circles; one rides a horse running in circles without progress. The arriving person is not a robber but a wife-seeker. But the girl would rather live a quiet and unmarried life for another ten years before she agrees to be married.

Six at the third line: Chasing a deer with no guide. As a result, the hunter becomes lost in the forest. He had better give up though he still expects to catch the deer. Should he go forward, he would be in great trouble.

Six at the fourth line: On the motionless horse, one pays court to a girl. Good fortune will prevail and everything will be advantageous.

Nine at the fifth line: To save oil. A small amount brings good luck whereas saving too much leads to disaster.

Six at the top line: One is on the back of a horse, hesitating without moving forward and weeping with continuous tears.

Notes:

1. 屯(zhun): originally meant new grass, wood, a spring seedling or the tree of heaven; here it signifies obstruction and difficulty.
2. 勿有用攸往(wu you yong you wang): do not start one's trip.
3. 建侯(jian hou): grant the title of duke or prince to someone.
4. 磐桓(pan huan): pace up and down.
5. 利居贞(li ju zhen): advantageous to be steadfastly faithful. 贞(zhen): steadfast faithfulness.
6. 屯如邅如(zhun ru zhan ru): being beset with difficulties and no way out at all. 屯(zhun): obstructed or in difficulty. 邅(zhan): go

around in circles.

7. 乘马班如(cheng ma ban ru): ride a horse, going in circles without progress. 班(ban): go round in circles.

8. 匪寇婚媾(fei kou hun gou): not a robber but a wife-seeker, 匪(fei): no; not.

9. 不字(bu zi): do not marry.

10. 即鹿无虞(ji lu wu yu): chase a deer without a guide. 即(ji): pursue, chase.

11. 君子几, 不如舍(jun zi ji, bu ru she): the gentleman expects to gain (the deer), but he had better give up the chase. 几(ji): approach, expect. 舍(she): give up, abandon.

12. 往吝(wang lin): in difficulties if one goes forward. 吝(lin): difficulty, trouble.

13. 屯其膏(tun qi gao): save oil. 屯(tun): save, gather, accumulate. 膏(gao): oil, grease, fat.

14. 小, 贞吉; 大, 贞凶(xiao, zhen ji; da, zhen xiong): small accumulation, good fortune; big accumulation, bad luck. 小(xiao): small, little.

15. 泣血涟如(qi xue lian ru): shed tears without stop. 泣血(qi xue): weep with no sound.

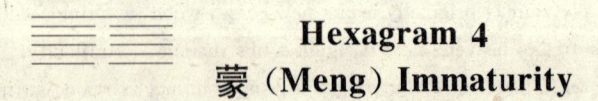

Hexagram 4
蒙 (Meng) Immaturity

The Chinese text:

蒙[1]。亨。匪我求童蒙[2], 童蒙求我。初筮告[3], 再三渎[4], 渎则不告。利贞[5]。
初六：发蒙, 利用刑人[6], 用说桎梏[7], 以往吝[8]。

10

九二：包蒙吉[9]，纳妇吉，子克家[10]。
六三：勿用取女[11]，见金夫，不有躬[12]，无攸利。
六四：困蒙，吝[13]。
六五：童蒙，吉[14]。
上九：击蒙。不利，为寇[15]；利，御寇[16]。

Translation：

  Immaturity: Good omen. It is not I who consult an immature youth, but the reverse. The first of his consultations will be answered with good or ill omen. However, the following ones will not, because repeated consultations of fortune are considered a blasphemy. This hexagram implies that one should keep the principle of steadfast faithfulness.

Six at the bottom line: When one trains an immature youth, one may use the condition of a prisoner to warn him. While the prisoner's fetters and handcuffs are off, he can go, but his actions are still limited.

Nine at the second line: Accepting the immaturity and innocence of youth is auspicious. It is advantageous for one to have a daughter-in-law and for one's son to establish a family.

Six at the third line: Do not marry this girl for she may lose her chastity when she meets a wealthy man. The marriage is unfavourable.

Six at the fourth line: Trapped by ignorance, one will certainly meet troubles.

Six at the fifth line: The child's naiveness and innocence signify good fortune.

Nine at the top line: The immature youth may become a robber or bandit if the training method is wrong. If right, he can be a defender against robbers or bandits.

Notes:

1. 蒙(meng): originally meant the grass and wood on high land, later referring to immaturity, unenlightenment or ignorance.

2. 非我求童蒙(fei wo qiu tong meng): not me to consult an immature youth. 童蒙(tong meng): naive and immature young person.

3. 初筮告(chu shi gao): give an answer to one's first consultation of divinaton. 初(chu): first, the first time. 筮(shi): do divination.

4. 再三渎(zai san du): repeated divinations are blasphemous. 渎(du): blaspheme, profane.

5. 利贞(li zhen): favourable to observe the principle of steadfast faithfulness. 贞(zhen): principle of steadfast faithfulness.

6. 发蒙,利用刑人(fa meng, li yong xing ren): take advantage of the prisoner's condition to enlighten the immature youth. 发(fa): enlighten, develop. 刑人(xing ren): prisoner, a person who is tortured.

7. 用说桎梏(yong tuo zhi ku): get rid of fetters and handcuffs. 说(tuo): deprive, get rid of. 桎梏(zhi ku): fetters and handcuffs.

8. 以往吝(yi wang lin): one has already gone, but he is still in difficulties. 以(yi): already. 吝(lin)is identical with 遴 here, meaning hard to move forward.

9. 包蒙吉(bao meng ji): accepting the immature youth is auspicious. 包(bao) was interpreted by some scholars as contain or involve. The interpretation here is in accord with classical Chinese references.

10. 纳妇吉,子克家(na fu ji, zi ke jia): it is auspicious to have a daughter-in-law and for one's son to make a family. 纳妇(na fu): seek a wife for one's son. 克(ke): make, establish, form.

11. 勿用取女(wu yong qu nu): do not marry this girl. 取(qu) is identical to 娶(qu), meaning to marry.

12. 见金夫,不有躬(jian jin fu, bu you gong): on meeting a wealthy man, she will lose her chastity. 金夫(jin fu): man with much money.

躬 (gong): body, chastity.

13. 困蒙, 吝 (kun meng, lin): being trapped in immaturity will certainly bring about a regrettable event.

14. 童蒙, 吉 (tong meng, ji): the child's immaturity indicates good fortune.

15. 击蒙, 不利, 为寇 (ji meng, bu li, wei kou): the immature youth will become a robber or bandit if the method of enlightenment is wrong. 击 (ji): treat, punish.

16. 利, 御寇 (li, yu kou): the right method can cause the immature one to become a defender against robbers or bandits.

Hexagram 5
需 (Xu) Waiting

The Chinese text:

需[1]：有孚[2]，光亨[3]，贞吉[4]。利涉大川[5]。
初九：需于郊，利用恒[6]，无咎。
九二：需于沙，小有言[7]，终吉。
九三：需于泥，致寇至[8]。
六四：需于血，出自穴[9]。
九五：需于酒食[10]，贞吉。
上六：入于穴，有不速之客三人来[10]；敬之，终吉。

Translation:

Waiting: Keep the principle of sincerity and faithfulness; offer sacrifices in various places. Good fortune. It is advantageous to cross great rivers.

Nine at the bottom line: Stay in the outskirts of the city and remain for some time. No disaster.

Nine at the second line: Sojourn on the sands. Some gossips and blames will arise but the end will be auspicious.

Nine at the third line: To wait in the mud will result in the arrival of robbers.

Six at the fourth line: Stay in the ditch and leave one's own dwelling place.

Nine at the fifth line: Refrain from food and drink. Good fortune.

Six at the top line: Three uninvited guests arrive when one returns to his own home. If he treats them with respect, a propitious outcome will follow.

Notes:

1. 需(xu): a sacrifice for rain in ancient times. It later came to mean waiting, inactivity or need.

2. 有孚(you fu): be sincere and faithful.

3. 光亨(guang heng): offer sacrifices in many places. 光(guang): widely, in various places. 亨(heng): offer a sacrifice to gods or ancestors.

4. 贞吉(zhen ji): good fortune. 贞(zhen): consult one's fortune by divination.

5. 利涉大川(li she da chan): advantageous to cross a great river. 大川(da chuan): great rivers.

6. 需于郊,利用恒(xu yu jiao, li yong heng): sojourn in the outskirts of the city and stay there for a long time. 郊(jiao): outskirts of a town or a city. 恒(heng): permanent or unchanging regulation.

7. 需于沙,小有言(xu yu sha, xiao you yan): stay on the sands and some gossips or blames arise. 小(xiao): a few, little. 言(yan): blames or condemnations.

8. 需于泥,致寇至(xu yu ni, zhi kou zhi): waiting in the mud results

in the coming of robbers. 寇(kou)：robber or bandit.

9. 需于血，出自穴 (xu yu xie, chu zi xue)：inactivity in a ditch; coming out of one's own dwelling place. 血(xie)：ditch. 穴(xue)：a cave in a mount or in the earth for a primitive to live in.

10. 需于酒食(xu yu jiu shi)：refrain from food and drink.

11. 不速之客(bu su zhi ke)：an uninvited guest. 速(su)：invite, call.

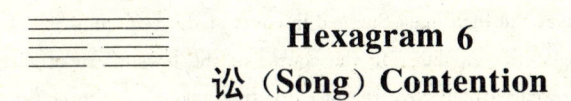

Hexagram 6
讼（Song）Contention

The Chinese text：

讼[1]：有孚，窒惕[2]。中吉，终凶[3]。利见大人。不利涉大川。

初六：不永所事[4]，小有言，终吉。

九二：不克讼[5]，归而逋[6]，其邑人三百户无眚[7]。

六三：食旧德[8]，贞厉[9]，终吉。或从王事，无成[10]。

九四：不克讼，复即命[11]，渝安贞[12]，吉。

九五：讼，元吉[13]。

上九：或锡之鞶带[14]，终朝三褫之[15]。

Translation：

Contention：Observe the principle of sincerity and faithfulness with repentance and fear. Sometimes there is passing success in the course of the contention, but it ends in disaster. It is advantageous to visit a great man but not to cross great rivers.

Six at the bottom line：Do not keep on at the contention. A little gossip occurs, but it brings good luck in the end.

Nine at the second line：No success in the court and one must escape as

15

soon as one returns home. No disasters befall the three hundred households of one's city.

Six at the third line: Share favours come down from the ancestors. The divination shows danger as well as good fortune in the end. To serve the monarch without clear aim leads to failure.

Nine at the fourth line: Not succeeding in the dispute, one goes back on one's words and submits oneself to destiny. It is auspicious to change one's initial intention and keep the principle of faithfulness.

Nine at the fifth line: Succeed in court at the beginning.

Nine at the top line: In the course of the lawsuit, an official belt is bestowed without clear reason; it is then taken away three times in the same day.

Notes:

1. 讼(song): a contention or a dispute.
2. 窒惕(zhi ti): repent and fear. 窒(zhi): regret or repent. 惕(ti): complain and fear.
3. 中吉，终凶(zhong ji, zhong xiong): sometimes favourable in the middle of the dispute, but disaster takes place in the end.
4. 不永所事(bu yong suo shi): do not keep on at the dispute. 永(yong): keep on, stick to, always. 事(shi): contention or dispute.
5. 不克讼(bu ke song): cannot win the dispute. 克(ke): win, success.
6. 归而逋(gui er bu): return and escape. 逋(bu): escape or flee.
7. 其邑人三百户无眚(qi yi ren san bai hu wu sheng): no calamities befall the three hundred households of the city. 邑(yi): town or city of ancient China. 眚(sheng): eye disease; refers to disaster or clamity in general.
8. 食旧德(shi jiu de): share favours come down from one's ancestors. 食(shi): enjoy, share. 旧德(jiu de): favours or grace from ancestors.
9. 贞厉(zhen li): this divination suggests danger.

10. 或从王事，无成 (huo cong wang shi, wu cheng): serve the king without clear aim and attain no success. 或 (huo) is here identical with 惑 (huo), with no clear aim.

11. 复即命 (fu ji ming): go back on one's word and submit oneself to destiny. 复 (fu): do not keep one's promise. 命 (ming): destiny, fate, lot.

12. 谕安贞 (yu an zhen): change one's initial intention and stick to the principle of steadfast faithfulness. 逾 (yu): change. 贞 (zhen): the principle of steadfast faithfulness.

13. 讼，元吉 (song, yuan ji): success in court at the beginning of the lawsuit. 元 (yuan): beginning, start, first.

14. 或锡之鞶带 (huo xi zhi pan dai): to be bestowed the official belt with no clear reason (in the court). 锡 (xi) is identical with 赐 (ci) here and means grant or bestow. 鞶 (pan): belt, girdle; the official belt in feudal China granted according to one's rank.

15. 终朝三褫之 (zhong zhao san chi zhi): the official belt was taken away thrice in a day. 褫 (chi): take away, deprive, take off.

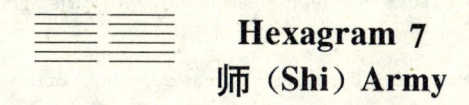

Hexagram 7
师 (Shi) Army

The Chinese text:

师[1]：贞丈人[2]。吉，无咎。
初六：师出以律[3]，否臧凶[4]。
九二：在师中[5]，吉，无咎。王三锡命[6]。
六三：师或舆尸[7]，凶。
六四：师左次[8]，无咎。

17

六五：田有禽，利执言[9]，无咎。长子帅师，弟子舆尸[10]，贞凶。
上六：大君有命[11]，开国承家[12]，小人勿用。

Traslation：

Army：Consult the commander of the army about its fortune. Good omen and no disaster.

Six at the bottom line：The army should follow musical cadence while marching forward or retreating; otherwise disasters may befall the army though the previous expedition was succesful.

Nine at the second line：The headquaters of the army is secure and powerful. Good fortune and no disaster. The king promulgates edicts to praise and encourage the commander and the army.

Six at the third line：The army was defeated because of hesitation and returned with waggons of corpses. Ill omen.

Six at the fourth line：There will be no harm if the army is camped on the left.

Six at the fifth line：It is auspicious to catch birds and beasts found in the fields. The elder son commanded the army to fight and the second son carried the bodies of the dead away with carts. This line shows misfortune.

Six at the top line：The monarch granted the titles of duke and allowed the establishment of thousand-waggoned kingdoms and granted to ministers the right to succeed to the hundred-waggoned clans. Do not count on the common persons.

Notes：

1. 师(shi) signifies a multitude or an army.
2. 贞丈人(zhen zhang ren)：ask the commander of the army about its fortune. 贞(zhen)：consult one's fortune. 丈人(zhang ren)：a person with noble character and great prestige; here denoting the commander

of the army.

3. 师出以律(shi chu yi lu): move with musical cadence when the army marches and fights. 律(lu): a musical rhythm used to direct the march or retreat of an army in ancient times.

4. 否臧凶(pi zang xiong): otherwise disaster will befall the army even if the previous expedition was triumphant. 否(pi): evil. It is written as 不(bu)in the *I Ching on Silk*, here meaning otherwise, or else. 臧(zang): slaves or servants; it also indicates goodness and the success of one's cause.

5. 在师中(zai shi zhong): in the centre of the army, describing the stable and powerful headquarters of the army.

6. 王三锡命(wang san xi ming): the king thrice issued edicts to praise the commander and the army. 锡(xi): grant, issue.

7. 师或舆尸(shi huo yu shi): to be rebuffed in the first battle and forced to retreat with waggons of corpses because of hesitation and no clear target.

8. 师左次(shi zuo ci): the army camps on the left. 次(ci): camp, station, settle.

9. 田有禽,利执言(tian you qin, li zhi yan): it is advantageous to catch the birds and beasts found in the fields. 田(tian): field or hunt, here meaning the former. 禽(qin): birds and beasts. 执(zhi): hold, catch.

10: 长子帅师,弟子舆师(zhang zi shuai shi, di zi yu shi): the elder son commanded the army to fight; the second son moved the dead with waggons. 长子(zhang zi): the elder son, denoting the commander here. 弟子(di zi): the second son.

11. 大君有命(da jun you ming): the monarch promulgates an edict to bestow noble titles according to one's achievments. 大君(da jun): emperor or king.

12. 开国承家(kai guo cheng jia): grant noble titles to establish thousand-waggoned kingdoms and grant high-ranked officials the right

to inherit the hundred-waggoned clans.

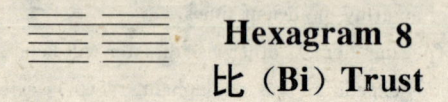

Hexagram 8
比（Bi）Trust

The Chinese text：

比¹，吉，原筮²，元永贞³，无咎。不宁方来，后夫凶⁴。
初六：有孚比之⁵，无咎。有孚盈缶⁶，终来有它⁷，吉。
六二：比之自内⁸，贞吉。
六三：比之匪人⁹。
六四：外比之¹⁰，贞吉。
九五：显比¹¹，王用三驱¹²，失前禽¹³，邑人不诫¹⁴，吉。
上六：比之无首¹⁵，凶。

Translation：

Trust：Good fortune. The second consultation of the oracles shows that one should, from the start and always, observe the principle of steadfast faithfulness. No disaster. The troublsome affairs follow one after another and the late-comer suffers from disaster.

Six at the bottom line：To have faithful and trusted followers results in no disaster. The faithful and trusted followers are as many as potfuls of wine. Good fortune although an accident happens in the end.

Six at the second line：The trusted and loyal followers come from within one's own circle. The oracle shows good omen.

Six at the third line：The trusted followers are not the right ones.

Six at the fourth line：It is auspicious to find faithful and trusted followers from outside of one's own circle.

Nine at the fifth line：Make the trusted followers known to the public.

The king chased game in a field with three sides enclosed and the front side open. The frontmost animal escaped. The people of the city did not fear. Good fortune.

Six at the top line: there is no leader among the faithful and trusted followers. Misfortune.

Notes:

1. 比(bi): close relation between two persons, denoting a trusted person or follower here.
2. 原筮(yuan shi): the second consultation of the oracle. (原): again, for the second time.
3. 元永贞(yuan yong zhen): always stick to the principle of steadfast faithfulness from the start.
4. 不宁方来，后夫凶(bu ning fang lai, hou fu xiong): the troublesome affairs come one after another and the last one to arrive suffers from disaster. 不宁(bu ning): troublesome, uneasy. 方来(fang lai): arrive or come continually. 后夫(hou fu): the late-comer or laggard.
5. 有孚比之(you fu bi zhi): be sincere and faithful to someone and have trusted followers. 孚(fu): sincere and faithful.
6. 有孚盈缶(you fu ying fou): sincere and faithful like a pot filled with wine. 缶(fou): clay wine container like a basin or pot.
7. 终来有它(zhong lai you tuo): an accident takes place in the end. 它(tuo): accident or unforeseen event.
8. 比之自内(bi zhi zi nei): the trusted follower comes from within one's own circle.
9. 比之匪人(bi zhi fei ren): the trusted person is not the right one. 匪(fei): not.
10. 外比之(wai bi zhi): find trusted followers from outside one's group.
11. 显比(xian bi): openly acknowlege the trusted persons.
12. 王用三驱(wang yong san qu): the king hunted by chasing game in

21

a field with three sides enclosed and the front side open.

13. 失前禽(shi qian qin): the game in the most frontward part escaped. In ancient times, when the king hunted, he usually left the front side open and pursued game from the other three sides. Therefore animals most frontward escaped easily.

14. 邑人不诫(yi ren bu jie): the people of the city do not fear.

15. 比之无首(bi zhi wu shou): there was no leader among the trusted persons.

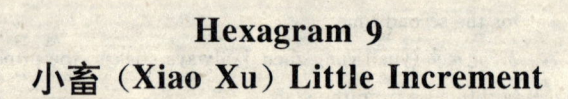

Hexagram 9
小畜 (Xiao Xu) Little Increment

The Chinese text:

小畜[1]：亨。密云不雨[2]，自我西郊[3]。
初九：复自道[4]，何其咎，吉。
九二：牵复[5]，吉。
九三：舆说辐[6]，夫妻反目[7]。
六四：有孚，血去惕出[8]，无咎。
九五：有孚挛如[9]，富以其邻[10]。
上九：既雨既处[11]，尚德载[12]，妇贞厉。月几望[13]，君子征凶。

Translation:

Little Increment: Good fortune. A dense cloud arises over the outskirts west of our town, but no rain.

Nine at the bottom line: What disaster will take place if one returns by oneself? Good fortune.

Nine at the second line: It is auspicious to be led back.

Nine at the third line: The wheel is off the cart. The husband and wife are staring angrily at each other.

Six at the fourth line: Be sincere and faithful, let go worries and horrible fears. No harm.

Nine at the fifth line: Maintain love with sincerity and faithfulness. Enrich oneself and do not forget about one's neighbours.

Nine at the top line: It has already rained and stopped, therefore, the carriage can go and carry things. It is a dangerous omen for women and not favourable to the superior man if he ventures on the sixteenth of every month.

Notes:

1. 小畜(xiao xu): little increment. 小(xiao): little, small amount. 畜(xu): save, accumulate or raise.

2. 密云不雨(mi yun bu yu): dense cloud without rain.

3. 自我西郊(zi wo xi jiao): the cloud arises over the western outskirts of our town.

4. 复自道(fu zi dao): return onself. 复(fu): return. 自道(zi dao): self-guiding.

5. 牵复(qian fu): being led back.

6. 舆说幅(yu tuo fu): the wheel and the cart are apart. 舆(yu): cart or waggon. 说(tuo): separate, take off. 幅(fu): the spoke of a wheel.

7. 夫妻反目(fu qi fan mu): husband and wife are angrily glaring at each other; indicating an inharmonious relation.

8. 血去惕出(xie qu ti chu): let go worry and fears. 血(xie): worry, anxiety. 惕(ti): fear, horror.

9. 有孚挛如(you fu luan ru): maintain love with sincerity and faithfulness. 挛(luan): love.

10. 富以其邻(fu yi qi lin): become rich with neighbours. 以(yi): togather, with.

11. 既雨既处(ji yu ji chu): the rain has already fallen and ceased. 既 (ji): already, finished. 处(chu): ceased or rested.

12. 尚德载(shang de zai): get a ride on someone's cart. 德(de): get, gain, aquire.

13. 月几望(yue ji wang): the day after the full moon. 几(ji): after. 几望(ji wang) is identical with 既望(ji wang), the sixteenth day of every lunar month.

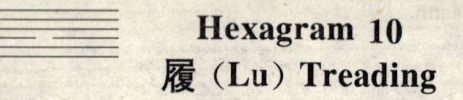

Hexagram 10
履 (Lu) Treading

The Chinese text:

履虎尾¹, 不咥人², 亨。

初九: 素履往³, 无咎。

九二: 履道坦坦⁴, 幽人贞吉⁵。

九三: 眇能视, 跛能履⁶, 履虎尾, 咥人凶, 武人为于大君⁷。

九四: 履虎尾, 愬愬, 终吉⁸。

九五: 夬履⁹, 贞厉。

上九: 视履考祥¹⁰, 其旋元吉¹¹。

Translation:

Treading: One treads on the tiger's tail, but it does not bite him. Good fortune.

Nine at the bottom line: No disaster if one goes there with white and unadorned shoes.

Nine at the second line: The path is level. It shows a good omen for a prisoner.

Six at the third line: A person with a blind eye can see and can walk on a lame leg. Treading on the tiger's tail, one is bitten. Misfortune. The military man ought to serve the king.

Nine at the fourth line: Treading on the tiger's tail with fear, one gets good result ultimately.

Nine at the fifth line: Go with no hesitation. The divination shows a danger in the future.

Nine at the top line: Looking to one's conduct and examining one's fortune, we know that one will not have good fortune unless one returns.

Notes:

1. 履虎尾(lu hu wei): treading on the tiger's tail. 履(lu)is written in the *I Ching on Silk* as 礼(li), meaning treading on or practise.

2. 不咥人(bu die ren): do not bite. 咥(die): bite, eat.

3. 素履往(su lu wang): go in white and unadorned shoes. 素履(su lu): white shoes with no adornment.

4. 履道坦坦(lu dao tan tan): the path is mostly level. 坦坦(tan tan): level, flat.

5. 幽人贞吉(you ren zhen ji): good omen for a prisoner. 幽人(you ren): prisoner.

6. 眇能视, 跛能履 (miao neng shi, po neng lu): see with one eye (the other is blind) and walk with one lame leg. 眇(miao): a person with one blind eye. 能(neng): can, and.

7. 武人为于大君(wu ren wei yu da jun): a military man serves the monarch.

8. 愬愬, 终吉 (su su, zhong ji): ultimately have good fortune though fear accompanies him. 愬愬(su su): in a fearful state.

9. 夬履(guai lu): go with no hesitation. 夬(guai): with no hesitation, with determination.

10. 视履考详(shi lu kao xiang): find out one's fortune by examining

one's conduct. 视(shi): examine and consider. 考(kao): examine and find out. 祥(xiang): good or bad fortune.

11. 其旋元吉(qi xuan yuan ji): no good fortune unless one returns. 旋(xuan): a circle without break, extending to return. It is written in the *I Ching on Silk* as 睘(huan), meaning return.

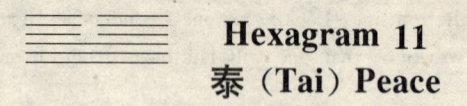

Hexagram 11
泰（Tai）Peace

The Chinese text:

泰[1]：小往大来[2]，吉，亨。

初九：拔茅茹以其汇[3]，征吉。

九二：包荒，用冯河[4]。不遐遗[5]，朋亡[6]，得尚于中行[7]。

九三：无平不陂，无往不复[8]，艰贞无咎[9]，勿恤其孚[10]，于食有福[11]。

六四：翩翩[12]，不富以其邻[13]，不戒以孚[14]。

六五：帝乙归妹以祉[15]，元吉。

上六：城复于隍[16]，勿用师，自邑告命[17]，贞吝[18]。

Translation:

Peace: Small loss and big gain. Good fortune.

Nine at the bottom line: uproot grasses but they are still attached to others of the same kind. Good fortune for one who commands an army.

Nine at the second line: Cross the great rivers and ford the long streams. Do not abandon a thing because it is far away. Be rewarded if one keeps the principle of the middle way.

Nine at the third line: There is no plain without slope and no going forth without return. One can avoid harm if one can observe the principle of steadfast faithfulness even if in difficulties. Do not worry over the return. This divination shows that one will enjoy good food.

Six at the fourth line: One goes to and fro and does not become rich with one's neighbours. One does not warn others in sincerity and faithfulness.

Six at the fifth line: King Yi was blessed for he arranged his daughter's marriage. Good fortune from the start.

Six at the top line: One cannot command the army to fight because the city wall has collapsed into the moat below it. One must offer sacrifice to heaven in the city. The divination indicates troubles.

Notes:

1. 泰(tai) is written as 柰 (nai) in the *I Ching on Silk*, meaning peace, good fortune and success.

2. 小往大来(xiao wang da lai): small loss and big gain (if one meets this hexagram).

3. 茹以其汇 (ru yi qi hui): the grass roots are attached to the surrounding similar ones. 茹(ru): root. 汇(hui): sort, kind.

4. 包荒，用冯河(bao huang, yong ping he): take advantage of the great river and ford the long stream. 包(bao): use, take advantage. 荒 (huang): great rivers, also written as 巟 in classical Chinese. 冯 (ping): ford, cross.

5. 不遐遗(bu xia yi): do not abandon it because it is far away. 遐 (xia): far, remote.

6. 朋亡(peng wang): do not forget. They are written as 弗忘(fu wang)in the *I Ching on Silk*, meaning do not forget.

7. 得尚于中行 (de shang yu zhong xing): rewards come from practising the principle of the middle way. 中行(zhong xing): walk in the middle of the road, extending to denote the principle of the middle way. 尚(shang) is identical with 赏(shang), meaning reward.

8. 无平不陂，无往不复(wu ping bu po, wu wang bu fu): there is no

plane without an incline and no going forth without return. 陂 (po): inclination. 复 (fu): return.

9. 艰贞无咎 (jian zhen wu jiu): harmless if one can keep the principle of righteousness in hard time. 艰 (jian): hard, difficulty. 贞 (zhen): faithful and righteous.

10. 勿恤其孚 (wu xu qi fu): do not worry about one's return. 恤 (xu): worry, anxiety. 孚 (fu) is identical with 復 (fu) which is found in the *I Ching on Silk*, meaning return.

11. 于食有福 (yu shi you fu): happy with delicious food.

12. 翩翩 (pian pian): the state of a flying bird, here signifying someone's frivolous conduct.

13. 不富以其邻 (bu fu yi qi lin): do not become rich with one's neighbours. 以 (yi): with, and.

14. 不戒以孚 (bu jie yi fu): do not warn someone in sincerity and faithfulness. 戒 (jie): warn.

15. 帝乙归妹以祉 (di yi gui mei yi zhi): King Yi was blessed for having his daughter married. 帝乙 (di yi): a king who is considered to be the father of King Zhou or King Cheng Tang. 归妹 (gui mei): a girl's marriage. 祉 (zhi): blessing, well-being.

16. 城复于隍 (cheng fu yu huang): the city wall collapsed into the moat. 复 (fu) is identical with 覆 (fu), meaning collapse. 隍 (huang): moat or ditch below the city wall.

17. 自邑告命 (zi yi gao ming): offer sacrifice in the city to heaven.

18. 贞吝 (zhen lin): the oracle shows one's troubles.

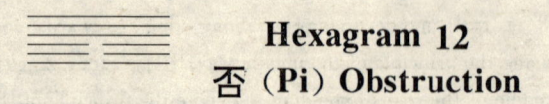

Hexagram 12
否 (Pi) Obstruction

The Chinese text:

否之匪人[1]，不利君子贞[2]，大往小来。
初六：拔茅茹以其汇，贞吉，亨。
六二：包承[3]，小人吉，大人否亨。
六三：包羞[5]。
九四：有命，无咎[6]。畴离祉[7]。
九五：休否[8]，大人吉。其亡其亡，系于苞桑[9]。
上九：倾否[10]，先否后喜。

Translation:

Obstruction: The obstructed one is not the person who deserves it. The hexagram shows disadvantage for a superior man. Big loss and small gain.

Six at the bottom line: Uproot the grasses and find them still attached to others of the same kind. The oracle indicates good fortune and success.

Six at the second line: The mean fellow prospers by flattery, while the superior man is obstucted.

Six at the third line: Accept the tribute.

Nine at the fourth line: No disaster follows because the king issued his edict. The multitude depend on each other and prosper together.

Nine at the fifth line: The superior man becomes succesful when the obstruction is removed. He would not have escaped death without planting mulberry.

Nine at the top line: The obstruction is gone. Bliss follows the removal of the obstruction.

Notes:

1. 否之匪人 (pi zhi fei ren): 否 (pi) is subsituted in the *I Ching on*

Silk by 妇(fu), signifying obstuction. The hexagram indicates that the blocked person should not be.

2. 不利君子贞(bu li jun zi zhen): the divination is unfavourable to a superior man.

3. 包承(bao cheng): succeed.

4. 大人否亨(da ren pi heng): the great man is in stagnation. 否(pi): not, negative.

5. 包羞(bao xiu): accept the tribute. 羞(xiu): tribute.

6. 有命,无咎(you ming, wu jiu): an edict was issued by the king. No disaster. 有命(you ming): accept orders or edicts from the king.

7. 畴离祉(chou li zhi): the multitude depend on each other and prosper together. 畴(chou): mass, multitude. 离(li): dependent. 祉(zhi): bliss, happiness, prosperity.

8. 休否(xiu pi): out of the obstruction. 休(xiu): stop, end.

9. 系于苞桑(xi yu bao sang): escape death because mulberry trees were planted. 苞(bao): plant.

10. 倾否(qing pi): the obstruction has collapsed; meaning the trouble is gone. 倾(qing): decline, collapse.

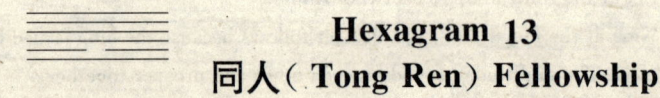

Hexagram 13
同人(Tong Ren) Fellowship

The Chinese text:

同人于野[1],亨。利涉大川,利君子贞。
初九:同人于门[2],无咎。
六二:同人于宗[3],吝。
九三:伏戎于莽[4],升其高陵[5],三岁不兴[6]。

九四：乘其墉，弗克攻[7]，吉。
九五：同人，先号咷而后笑[8]，大师克相遇[9]。
上九：同人于郊[10]，无悔。

Translation:

Fellowship: Unite people and have fellowship in the open fields. Good fortune. It is favourable for a superior man to cross great rivers and practise the principle of steadfast faithfulness.

Nine at the bottom line: There is no disaster if one unites people and creates fellowship beyond the confines of one's gate.

Six at the second line: One will be in difficulties if one unites people and has fellowship only within his own clan.

Nine at the third line: Having hidden the army in the forest and observed the surroundings from the high hill, one finds that one should not send the army to fight in the following three years.

Nine at the fourth line: Climb to the top of the city wall but do not attack the enemy any more. Good fortune.

Nine at the fifth line: Unite the people and make concerted efforts to attack the enemy, loudly crying out at first and later laughing when the soldiers meet after their occupation of the city.

Nine at the top line: To unite the people and make friends in the outskirts of the city does not lead to regret.

Notes:

1. 同人于野 (tong ren yu ye): to unite people and make friends in the open fields beyond the outskirts of the city. 同人 (tong ren) means to unite people and make friends, find or gather persons. 野 (ye): open fields. In classical Chinese, the place close to a city is called the outskirts and the open beyond the outskirts is called open field.

2. 同人于门 (tong ren yu men): find fellows outside the gate. 于门

(yu men): beyond the limitation of one's gate.

3. 同人于宗，吝 (tong ren yu zong, lin): troubles will follow if one unites the people and has friends only within one's own clan. 宗 (zong): clan. 吝 (lin): in touble or in difficulty.

4. 伏戎于莽 (fu rong yu mang): to camp the army in the woods. 戎 (rong): army. 莽 (mang): woods or forest.

5. 升其高陵 (sheng qi gao ling): to climb to the high hill to observe the surroundings. 升 (sheng): climb, mount. It is written as 登 (deng) in the *I Ching on Silk*.

6. 三岁不兴 (san sui bu xing): do not dispatch army for three years. 岁 (sui): year.

7. 乘其墉，弗克攻 (cheng qi yong, fu ke gong): to mount the top of the city wall but not to attack. 乘 (cheng): to climb and occupy. 墉 (yong): city wall.

8. 同人，先号咷而后笑 (tong ren, xian hao tao er hou xiao): to work together with one will; cry at first and then laugh. 号咷 (hao tao): loudly cry with tears.

9. 大师克相遇 (da shi ke xiang yu): the great army comes together when it occupies the city. 大师 (da shi): the great army.

10. 同人于郊 (tong ren yu jiao): to unite people and have close relations with them in the outskirts.

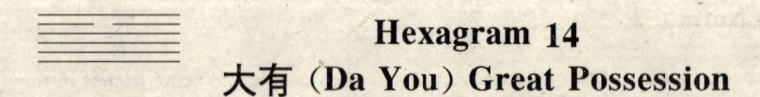

Hexagram 14
大有（Da You）Great Possession

The Chinese text:

大有[1]：元亨。

32

初九：无交害。匪咎艰则无咎²。
九二：大车以载，有攸往³，无咎。
九三：公用亨于天子，小人弗克⁴。
九四：匪其彭⁵，无咎。
六五：厥孚交如，威如⁶，吉。
上九：自天祐之⁷，吉，无不利。

Translation：

Great Possession：One is succesful from the beginning.

Nine at the bottom line：It is not damaged seriously. There would be no disaster if its cause is removed.

Nine at the second line：To carry things to a destination with great waggons. No harm.

Nine at the third line：The duke payed tribute to the Emperor but ordinary persons were not in the same position.

Nine at the fourth line：It is harmless not to show pride for one's greatness.

Six at the fifth line：Sincere and faithful friendship is deeply respected. Good fortune.

Nine at the top line：Being blessed by Heaven, nothing is unfavourable.

Notes：

1. 大有(da you)：great possession, multitude or considerably wealthy. In ancient China, the people called a year with good harvest 有(you), a rich year; 大有(da you) denoted the richest year or the year with the greatest harvest.

2. 无交害。匪咎艰则无咎(wu jiao hai. fei jiu jian ze wu jiu)：not damage the essential part. There will be no disaster if no cause of it exists. 匪(fei)：no, not. 艰(jian)：root, cause or origin. In the *I*

Ching On Silk, it is written as 根(gen), meaning root.

3. 大车以载,有攸往(da che yi zai, you you wang): to carry things with great waggons to a destination.

4. 公用亨于天子,小人弗克(gong yong heng yu tian zi, xiao ren fu ke): the duke pays tribute to the emperor whereas the ordinary people cannot. 亨(heng) is identical with 享(xiang), meaning paying tribute; in the *I Ching On Silk* it is written as 芳(fang), identical in meaning with 享.

5. 匪其彭(fei qi pang): does not involve arrogance because of one's greatness. 匪(fei): no, not. 彭(pang): great, enomous.

6. 厥孚交如,威如(jue fu jiao ru, wei ru): the sincere and faithful friendship is deeply respected. 厥(jue): the, one's. 孚(fu): sincerity and faithfulness. 威(wei): authorative and respectful.

7. 自天祐之(zi tian you zhi): blessed by Heaven. 祐(you): bless.

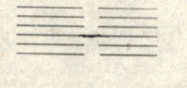

Hexagram 15
谦(Qian) Modesty

The Chinese text:

谦[1]:亨,君子有终[2]。

初六:谦谦君子[3],用涉大川,吉。

六二:鸣谦[4],贞吉。

九三:劳谦[5],君子有终,吉。

六四:无不利,㧑谦[6]。

六五:不富以其邻,利用侵伐[7],无不利。

上六:鸣谦,利用行师,征邑国[8]。

34

Translation:

Modesty: Good omen. The superior man has a good end.

Six at the bottom line: It is auspicious for the superior man, who is always modest and prudent, to cross great rivers. Good fortune.

Six at the second line: Good luck to the person who can remain modest even though he possesses great fame.

Nine at the third line: The person who is not arrogant of his achievment will have a good end in life. Good omen.

Six at the fourth line: To practise and develop modesty ensures success in everything.

Six at the fifth line: It is auspicious to take military action against those who do not become rich together with their neighbours.

Six at the top line; one who can remain modest despite being well-known is in an advantageous position to send forces to punish his neighbouring kingdom.

Notes:

1. 谦(qian): modesty, politeness.
2. 君子有终(jun zi you zhong): the superior man has a good end. 有终 (you zhong): have a good end.
3. 谦谦君子(qian qian jun zi): a very modest and prudent gentleman. 谦谦(qian qian): rather modest and prudent.
4. 鸣谦(ming qian): remain modest in spite of one's good reputation. 鸣(ming): good reputation.
5. 劳谦(lao qian): be modest despite one's great achievements. 劳 (lao): achievement.
6. 扐谦 (hui qian): practise and develop one's modesty. 扐 (hui) originally meant tear or split; here it represents practise or develop.
7. 不富以其邻,利用侵伐(bu fu yi qi lin, li yong qin fa): those who

do not enrich together with their neighbours deserve suppression.

8. 利用行师,征邑国(li yong xing shi, zheng yi guo): to send military force to attack and suppress the kingdom of a duke. 征(zheng): take military attack and punishment.

Hexagram 16
豫(Yu) Enjoyment

The Chinese text:

豫[1]:利建侯,行师[2]。
初六:鸣豫[3],凶。
六二:介于石,不终日,贞吉。
六三:盱豫[5],悔;迟,有悔[6]。
九四:由豫,大有得[7],勿疑,朋盍簪[8]。
六五:贞疾,恒不死[9]。
上六:冥豫,成有渝[10],无咎。

Translation:

Enjoyment: It is advantageous to found a kingdom and take military action.

Six at the bottom line: One is well known for enjoying pleasures. Misfortune.

Six at the second line: Observe the principle of steadfast faithfulness like an unmovable rock. Good fortune.

Six at the third line: Flattery results in regret and hesitation brings regret, too.

Nine at the fourth line: While enjoying pleasures and having abundance, one avoids hesitation. Gather friends.

Six at the fifth line: Consult an oracle about one's illness. It shows that the disease will last long before death.

Six at the top line: Still indulge in sensual pleasures after sunset. Succeed and a change will occur in the end but no disaster follows.

Notes:

1. 豫(yu): enjoyment, indulgence, weariness, originally meaning the size of an elephant. It is written as 余 (yu) in the *I Ching on Silk* and means entertainment.

2. 利建侯, 行师(li jian hou, xing shi): good time to establish a kingdom and take military action. 侯(hou): kingdom of a duke or prince. 行师(xing shi): take military action.

3. 鸣豫 (ming yu): famous for enjoying something pleasing. 鸣 (ming): fame, famous.

4. 介于石, 不终日, 贞吉(jie yu shi, bu zhong ri, zhen ji): to be steadfast with no daily change like an immoveable rock. Good fortune. 介(jie): firm, steadfast and righteous.

5. 盱豫, 悔(xu yu, hui): regret comes from looking up and flattering a powerful personage. 盱 (xu): to open one's eyes, derogatorily signifying pride and confidence.

6. 迟, 有悔(chi, you hui): hesitation brings regret. 迟(chi): hesitation.

7. 由豫, 大有得(you yu, da you de): enjoy pleasures and become abundantly wealthy. 由豫(you yu): enjoy and indulge in pleasures. 大有得(da you de): enormously abundant and rich.

8. 勿疑, 朋盍簪(wu yi, peng he zan): so faithful as not to suspect; friends gather. 勿(wu): do not do. 朋(peng): friend. 盍(he): gather or assemble. 簪(zan) is a needle-like ornament worn by women to hold up their hair; here it menans link, connect.

9. 贞疾, 恒不死(zhen ji, heng bu si): consult a divination about one's

diseases, which are chronic and will last a long time before one's death. 贞(zhen): divination. 疾(ji): illness, diseases. 恒(heng): permanent, abiding, eternal.

10. 冥豫，成有渝(ming yu, cheng you yu): still indulge in pleasure when the sun has set. Success sometimes but an unfortunate change will take place in the end. 冥(ming): the time of sunset; dark. 渝(yu): change, occurence.

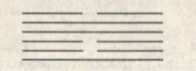

Hexagram 17
随(Sui) Following

The Chinese text:

随[1]，元亨，利贞[2]，无咎。
初九：官有渝，贞吉[3]，出门交有功[4]。
六二：系小子，失丈夫[5]。
六三：系丈夫，失小子。随有求得。利居贞[6]。
九四：随有获，贞凶[7]。有孚在道，以明，何咎[8]？
九五：孚于嘉[9]，吉。
上六：拘系之，乃从维之，王用亨于西山[10]。

Translation:

Following: One should keep the principle of steadfast faithfulness if one starts with success. No disaster.

Nine at the bottom line: Changes happen to the house; good omen. One will be benefited by one's social activities outside the home.

Six at the second line: While holding the child, the adult left.

Six at the third line: Holding the adult, losing the child. It is right to stay at home and remain faithful when one follows others and gains what one desires.

Nine at the fourth line: One is given an ill omen when one follows others and achieves what one wants; however, what disaster will there be if one has been faithful and taken an oath to be so?

Nine at the fifth line: Be faithful to the good and beautiful. Good fortune.

Six at the top line: Imprisoned first and set free later. As a result, the king makes offerings on West Mountain.

Notes:

1. 随(sui): to follow; to be in harmony with someone.
2. 元亨,利贞(yuan heng, li zhen): the initial success suggests that one should persist in the principle of steadfast faithfulness. 元(yuan): beginning, initial. 亨(heng): success, without obstruction. 贞(zhen): remain faithful to someone.
3. 官有渝, 贞吉(guan you yu, zhen ji): change one's house. Good omen. 官(guan) is identical with 馆(guan), denoting all kinds of houses.
4. 出门交有功(chu men jiao you gong): satisfying result comes from social intercourse outside the home. 交(jiao): social activities.
5. 系小子,失丈夫(ji xiao zi, shi zhang fu): the adult escapes when you hold the child. 系(ji): hold, bind, tite. 小子(xiao zi): teenager, child. 丈夫(zhang fu): adult, man.
6. 随有求得,利居贞(sui you qiu de, li ju zhen): to follow someone and gain what one desires. Auspicious to be faithful at home. 随(sui): to follow.
7. 随有获,贞凶(sui you huo, zhen xiong): to follow and achieve. Ill omen. 获(huo) was a derogatory name for slaves and servants in ancient China; here it means gain or achieve.
8. 有孚在道, 以明, 何咎(you fu zai dao, yi ming, he jiu): what

disaster will happen if one remains faithful and has sworn to do so. 明 (ming) is identical with 盟(ming), meaning swear or take an oath.

9. 孚于嘉(fu yu jia): faithful to the good and beautiful. 嘉(jia): good and beautiful.

10. 拘系之,乃从维之,王用亨于西山(ju ji zhi, nai cong wei zhi, wang yong heng yu xi shan): imprisoned first and then set free. The king offered a sacrifice on West Mountain. 拘系(ju ji): imprison someone. 从维(cong wei): release, set free. 亨(heng): in the earliest Chinese, it is drawn like a picture of a temple, signifying the acceptance and enjoyment of offerings.

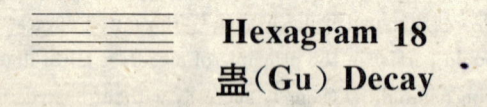

Hexagram 18
蛊(Gu) Decay

The Chinese text:

蛊[1]：元亨，利涉大川。先甲三日，后甲三日[2]。
初六：干父之蛊，有子，考无咎[3]。厉，终吉。
九二：干母之蛊，不可贞[4]。
九三：干父之蛊，小有悔[5]，无大咎。
六四：裕父之蛊，往见吝[6]。
六五：干父之蛊，用誉[7]。
上九：不事王侯，高尚其事[8]。

Translation:

Decay: One starts with success. It will be favourable to cross great rivers in the three days before or after the first day of each of the Heavenly Stems.

40

Six at the bottom line: The father can avert disasters if he has a son who can correct his mistakes in time. Though the father faces danger sometimes, he unquestionably ends well.

Nine at the second line: Do not stubbornly insist on the principle of faithfulness when treating one's mother's mistakes.

Nine at the third line: One is not seriously wrong for correcting one's father's faults though one slightly regrets it.

Six at the fourth line: One will still feel shame to see one's father, even if one leniently dealt with the father's errors.

Six at the fifth line: Correct one's father's mistakes by means of one's honour.

Nine at the top line: Do not serve the king or princes. Keep yourself morally pure.

Notes:

1. 蛊(gu): originally meant decayed food with many insects held in a container; here it means a mess, confusion, perplexity and also mistake, fault, error.

2. 先甲三日，后甲三日(xian jia san ri, hou jia san ri): the ancient Chinese recorded the days according to the cycle of the ten Heavenly Stems, ten day period which were repeated. The interpretation is: three days before the first; three days after the first.

3. 干父之蛊，有子，考无咎(gan fu zhi gu, you zi, kao wu jiu): the father will have no disaster if he has a son who can correct his mistakes. 干(gan): correct, save. 考(kao): a formal name for father. The ancient Chinese called their living or dead father this name.

4. 干母之蛊，不可贞(gan mu zhi gu, bu ke zhen): do not stubbornly follow the principle of faithfulness when correcting one's mother's faults.

5. 小有悔(xiao you hui): regret slightly. 小(xiao): little, small, slightly; it is written in the *I Ching on Silk* as 少(shao) with the same

meaning. 悔(hui): regret.

6. 裕父之蛊，往见吝(yu fu zhi gu, wang jian lin): still feels shamed when seeing one's father even if one has leniently dealt with the father's mistakes. 裕（yu）: mild, lenient. 吝（lin）: a shame or humiliation.

7. 干父之蛊，用誉(gan fu zhi gu, yong yu): correct one's father's mistake with one's honour. 用（yong）: by means of, in virtue of. 誉（yu）: honour, fame, glory.

8. 不事王侯，高尚其事(bu shi wang hou, gao shang qi shi): do not serve the king or princes. Keep oneself morally high.

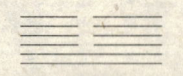

Hexagram 19
临(Lin) Looking Down

The Chinese text:

临[1]：元亨，利贞。至于八月有凶[2]。
初九：咸临，贞吉[3]。
九二：咸临，吉，无不利。
六三：甘临，无攸利[4]。既忧之，无咎[5]。
六四：至临，无咎[6]。
六五：知临，大君之宜[7]，吉。
上六：敦临[8]，吉，无咎。

Translation:

Looking Down: Started with success, one should stay to the principle of faithfulness. Misfortune will take place in the eighth month.

Nine at the bottom line: Good fortune for someone who can rule the people with humanity.

Nine at the second line: Nothing will be unfavourable if one rules the people with humanity.

Six at the third line: No favourable result comes if one rules the people with only honeyed tongue and sugared words. There will be no disaster if one is aware of and worries about it.

Six at the fourth line: Approach the people and understand their real situation. No harm.

Six at the fifth line: The monarch knows what he should do and can rule the people with wisdom. Good fortune.

Six at the top line: Good luck ensues if one can rule the people sincerely. No disaster.

Notes:

1. 临(lin): It originally meant looking down from above; by extension it refers to proceed and govern or rule; here it means rule. In the *I Ching on Silk* it is written as 林(lin).

2. 至于八月有凶(zhi yu ba yue you xiong): misfortune will arrive in the eighth month.

3. 咸临，贞吉(xian lin, zhen ji): govern the people with humanity. Good fortune. 咸 (xian) is identical with 感(gan), meaning feeling, emotion.

4. 甘临，无攸利(gan lin, wu you li): no favourable result comes if one governs the people with only honeyed tongue and sugared words. 甘(gan): sweet phrases and expressions.

5. 既忧之，无咎(ji you zhi, wu jiu): having been aware of and worried about it, one can avoid misfortune. 既(ji): already.

6. 至临，无咎(zhi lin, wu jiu): come down and know the real situation of the people. No harm. 至(zhi): come down.

7. 知临，大君之宜(zhi lin, da jun zhi yi): it is appropriate for a king to rule the people with wisdom.

8. 敦临(dun lin): rule the people with a sincere manner. 敦(dun): sincerity.

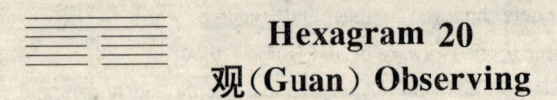

Hexagram 20
观(Guan) Observing

The Chinese text:

观¹：盥而不荐²，有孚颙若³。
初六：童观⁴，小人无咎，君子吝。
六二：闚观，利女贞⁵。
六三：观我生，进退⁶。
六四：观国之光，利用宾于王⁷。
九五：观我生，君子无咎。
上九：观其生，君子无咎⁸。

Translation:

Observing: Clean yourself before making an offering by washing hands. You do not need to offer drink and food for sacrifice. The manner of faithfulness and respect is admirable.

Six at the bottom line: To observe things in a childish way is accepable for an ordinary man but not a superior man. If a superior man acts so, he cannot attain his great goal.

Six at the second line: Peeking out though the crack of the door, the woman should stick to the principle of sincerity and faithfulness.

Six at the third line: Observe and inspect my own people in order to make the right decision in governing policy.

Six at the fourth line: When inspecting the people's costumes and practices of a country, the minister should meet the king according to appropriate ceremony.

Nine at the fifth line: No disaster will befall the superior man who has inspected his own people.

Nine at the top line: Inspecting the people of other countries, the superior man faces no calamity.

Notes:

1. 观(guan): look, observe, inspect.
2. 盥而不荐(guan er bu jian): wash your hands and clean yourself instead of making an offering. 盥(guan): the ceremony of washing hands before offering in ancient China. 荐(jian): to offer drink and food as sacrifices.
3. 有孚颙若(you fu yong ruo): the appearance of faithfulness and admiration. 孚(fu): sincerity and faithfulness. 颙若(yong ruo): respect and admire.
4. 童观(tong guan): observe in a childish way.
5. 阚观,利女贞(kui guan, li nu zhen): peek out through the crack of the door. It is proper for women to be sincere and faithful. 阚(kui): look out through the crack of the door in secret.
6. 观我生,进退(guan wo sheng, jin tui): to observe my people and then know when to advance or retreat (in governing policy). 生(sheng) means ordinary people here.
7. 观国之光,利用宾于王(guan guo zhi guang, li yong bin yu wang): inspecting the people's costumes and practices of the country one should interview the king with appropriate ceremony. 国之光(guo zhi guang): costumes and practices of the people in a country.
8. 观其生(guan qi sheng): to observe and inspect the people of other countries.

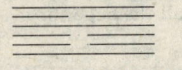

Hexagram 21
噬嗑(Shi He) Biting

The Chinese text

噬嗑[1]：亨，利用狱[2]。
初九：屦校灭趾[3]，无咎。
六二：噬肤灭鼻[4]，无咎。
六三：噬腊肉，遇毒，小吝[5]，无咎。
九四：噬乾胏，得金矢，利艰贞[6]，吉。
六五：噬乾肉，得黄金，贞厉[7]，无咎。
上九：何校灭耳[8]，凶。

Translation：

Biting：Sublime success. It is advantageous to deal with legal affairs.

Nine at the bottom line：The feet were covered by the instruments of torture. No disaster.

Six at the second line：One bites meat so deeply that it covers one's nose. No harm.

Six at the third line：One was poisoned after having eaten dried meat. A little trouble arises but no disaster.

Nine at the fourth line：One found a brass arrow when one had meat with bone in it. It suggests that one remains sincere and faithful when in difficulties.

Six at the fifth line：One came upon a piece of brass when eating dried meat. The divination shows danger but no disaster.

Nine at the top line：One is chained with such a big neck yoke that it covers one's ears. Misfortune.

Notes:

1. 噬嗑(shi he): bite through. 噬(shi) means to gnaw, bite. 嗑(he) means to bite through till the teeth touch. In this hexagram it signifies penalty.

2. 利用狱(li yong yu): favourable to deal with legal affairs. 狱(yu): law; legal affairs.

3. 屦校灭趾(lu xiao mie zhi): feet are chained by fetters and the toes are covered by them. 屦(lu) is identical with 履(lu), to put on one's feet. 校(xiao) is the general name for instruments of torture including handcuffs and fetters. 灭(mie): to cover or bury.

4. 噬肤灭鼻(shi fu mie bi): to bury one's nose into the meat when one eats it. 噬(shi): bite, eat. 肤(fu): meat; especialy the soft part with some fat.

5. 噬腊肉，遇毒，小吝(shi la rou, yu du, xiao lin): having eaten dried meat, one was poisoned. Small misfortune. 腊(la): dried meat. In ancient Chinese rites, there were specialists for making dried meat.

6. 噬乾胏，得金矢，利艰贞(shi gan zi, de jin shi, li jian zhen): to eat meat with bone and find the brass-made arrow indicates that one should stay sincere and faithful in hard times. 乾(gan): dry or dried. 胏(zi): meat with bone. 金(jin): brass, bronze, copper.

7. 噬乾肉，得黄金，贞厉(shi gan rou, de huang jin, zhen li): while eating dried meat one bites the yellow brass of the arrow. The divination shows danger. 厉(li): danger.

8. 何校灭耳(he xiao mie er): one's neck is held by a yoke which is so big as to cover one's ears. 何(he) is identical with 荷(he), meaning to carry. 校(xiao) here means cangue or neck yoke, an instrument of torture.

Hexagram 22
贲(Bi) Adornment

The Chinese text:

贲[1]:亨,小利有攸往[2]。
初九:贲其趾,舍车而徒[3]。
六二:贲其须[4]。
九三:贲如濡如,永贞吉[5]。
六四:贲如皤如,白马翰如[6],匪寇婚媾[7]。
六五:贲于丘园,束帛戋戋[8],吝,终吉。
上九:白贲[9],无咎。

Translation:

Adornment: Great success. A little benefit awaits. One can go there.
Nine at the bottom line: Adorning the feet, one would rather walk on foot instead of taking carriage.
Six at the second line: Adorn one's moustache and beard.
Nine at the third line: Decorated and glistening while staying steadfast and faithful. Good fortune will follow.
Six at the fourth line: Decorated with white, the horse runs as a bird flies. They are not robbers, but wife-seekers.
Six at the fifth line: Decorate the houses and garden with only a little silk cloth; it appears too simple, but ends well.
Nine at the top line: Decorating with white; no fault.

Notes:

1. 贲(bi): adornment, decoration. It is written in the *I Ching on Silk*

as 繁(fan).

2. 小利有攸往(xiao li you you wang): small benefit awaits; you can go there for it.

3. 贲其趾，舍车而徒(bi qi zhi, she che er xi): one leaves his carriage and walks on foot because of the adornment of his toes. 趾(zhi): toes. 徒(xi): walk.

4. 贲其须(bi qi xu): decorate the moustache and beard. 须(xu) is identical with 鬚; denoting all face hair including moustache and beard.

5. 贲如濡如，永贞吉(bi ru ru ru, yong zhen ji): decorated and glistening, one may have good fortune if one remains steadfast and faithful. 濡(ru): damp and glistening. 永(yong): always, permanent. 贞(zhen): steadfast and faithful.

6. 贲如皤如，白马翰如(bi ru po ru, bai ma han ru): adorned with white, the white horse runs as fast as a flying bird. 皤(po): white hair of the aged, here denoting a white appearance. 翰如(han ru): the horse runs like a flying bird.

7. 匪寇婚媾(fei kou hun gou): the arriving person is not a robber but a wife seeker. 匪(fei): no, not. 寇(kou): robber or bandit.

8. 贲于丘园，束帛戋戋 (bi yu qiu yuan, shu bo jian jian): decorate a house and garden only with a little silk clothing. 丘园(qiu yuan): home with a garden. 帛(bo): cloth made of silk. 戋戋(jian jian) is identical with 残残(can can), meaning a little, a few.

9: 白贲(bai bi): adorn with white colour.

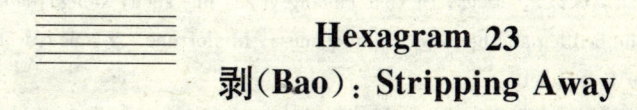

Hexagram 23
剥(Bao): Stripping Away

The Chinese text:

49

剥[1]：不利有攸往。
初六：剥床以足、蔑贞，凶[2]。
六二：剥床以辨[3]，蔑贞，凶。
六三：剥之，无咎。
六四：剥床以肤[4]，凶。
六五：贯鱼以宫人宠[5]，无不利。
上九：硕果不食，君子得舆，小人剥庐[6]。

Translation：

Stripping Away：It is not advantageous to go anywhere.

Six at the bottom line：Break the leg of the bed and lose righteousness. Misfortune.

Six at the second line：Damage the frame of the bed and lose righteousness. Dangerous.

Six at the third line：Damage but no loss.

Six at the fourth line：One's skin is hurt when one breaks the bed. Misfortune.

Six at the fifth line：The favourite concubines enter the room like a string of fishes. Nothing is unfavourable.

Nine at the top line：The biggest fruit is not eaten. The superior man will gain carriages whereas the little man will lose his hut.

Notes：

1. 剥(bao)：strip, damage or erode.
2. 剥床以足，蔑贞，凶 (bao chuang yi zu, mie zhen, xiong)：damage the bed leg and be rid of righteousness. Misfortune. 蔑(mie)：destroy or be extinct.
3. 剥床以辨(bao chuang yi bian)：break the frame of the bed. 辨(bian)：bed frame.
4. 剥床以肤(bao chuang yi fu)：one hurts one's skin when one

damages the frame of bed. 肤(fu): human skin or surface of the bed frame; here it means the former.

5. 贯鱼以宫人宠(guan yu yi gong ren chong): the favorite concubines in the palace enter one after another like a string of fishes. 贯(guan): link someting with a string. 贯鱼（guan yu): to string fishes, describing the concubines entering the mansion one after another. 宫人 (gong ren): concubines in the palace.

6. 硕果不食，君子得舆，小人剥庐(shou guo bu shi, jun zi de yu, xiao ren bao lu): The biggest fruit is not eaten. The superior man will gain carriages and the small man will have his hut damaged. 舆（yu): carriage. 庐(lu): house, hut.

Hexagram 24
复(Fu) Return

The Chinese text:

复[1]：亨，出入无疾[2]，朋来无咎[3]。反复其道[4]，七日来复[5]，利有攸往。
初九：不远复，无祗悔[6]，元吉。
六二：休复[7]，吉。
六三：频复[8]，厉，无咎。
六四：中行独复[9]。
六五：敦复，无悔。
上六：迷复，凶，有灾眚[11]。用行师，终有大败，以其国君凶，至于十年不克征[12]。

Translation:

Return: Great success. No illness when leaving or returning and no disaster while friends come. Returning to the original way takes the traveler seven days. Hence it is advantageous to go somewhere.

Nine at the bottom line: One returns before going too far. Therefore no serious trouble is brought about. It is auspicious from the beginning.

Six at the second line: Correct mistakes and return to the right way. Good fortune.

Six at the third line: Frequent returns indicates danger but not disaster.

Six at the fourth line: Return alone by walking in the middle of the path.

Six at the fifth line: Return when urged. No regret.

Six at the top line: Trying to return after going astray. Misfortune but no imminent calamity. To use a marching army to fight one will be terribly defeated and put the monarch in such a difficult situation that he will not be able to take military action in the following ten years.

Notes:

1. 复(fu): return.
2. 出入无疾(chu ru wu ji): going forth or coming back is free from illness. 疾(ji): illness, disease.
3. 朋来无咎(peng lai wu jiu): friends come in peace.
4. 反复其道(fan fu qi dao): return to the right way. 反(fan): go back. 复(fu): return.
5. 七日来复(qi ri lai fu): there are various interpretations for these words. The first is: the active force arises and ends in hexagram *Bao* (Stripping Away) and regenerates in hexagram *Fu* (Return) which lasts for seven days. The second is: the passive force occurs in hexagram *Gou* (meeting) of May and the active force takes place in hexagram *Fu* (Return) of November. During this period of seven months, changes happen seven times. The last is: take away from the sixty-four hexagrams the following four hexagrams *Kan*, *Zhen*, *Li* and *Dui*, each

of which consists of six lines, and let them to stand for the Twenty-four Solar Terms. Thus the 360 lines of the remaining sixty hexagrams represent 360 and 1/4 days and each hexagram represents 6 days and 7 minutes. Therefore we have the following formula:

365 and 1/4 days × 1/60 = 6 and 7/80 days

This is very close to seven days and therefore explains the origin of " seven days " in the sentence. Among these three interpretations, we consider the first most acceptable.

6. 不远复，无祇悔(bi yuan fu, wu qi hui): having returned before going too far and thus averted serious regret. 祇(qi): great, much, very, too. In the *I Ching on Silk*, it is written as 提(ti), identical with 禔(ti). These three characters can be substituted with each other in classical Chinese.

7. 休复(xiu fu): stop and return (to the righteous way). 休(xiu): stop, end or beautiful, joyful and jubilant; here means stop or end.

8. 频复(pin fu): frequent returns. 频(pin): frequent, often; it is written in the *I Ching on Silk* as 编(bian).

9. 中行独复(zhong xing du fu): walk in the middle of the path, and return alone. 中行(zhong xing): to walk in the middle of the path.

10. 敦复(dun fu): return when pressed. 敦(dun): press, urge or sincerity; here means the former.

11. 迷复，凶，有灾眚(mi fu, xiong, you zai sheng): going astray and then trying to return. Ill omen and disaster comes. 眚(sheng)indicates disaster here.

12. 用行师，终有大败，以其国君凶，至于十年不克征(yong xing shi, zhong you da bai, yi qi guo jun xiong, zhi yu shi nian bu ke zheng): to fight with a marching army and be defeated terribly which brings serious troubles to the king so that he will not be able to send military force again in the next ten years. 以(yi): and. 不克征(bu ke zheng): cannot send force to fight.

Hexagram 25
无妄（Wu Wang）The Unexpected

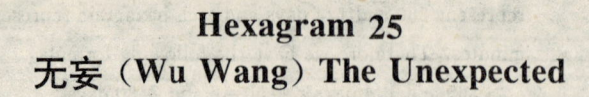

The Chinese text：

无妄[1]：元亨利贞。其匪正有眚[2]，不利有攸往。
初九：无妄，往吉。
六二：不耕获，不菑畬[3]，则利有攸往。
六三：无妄之灾，或系之牛，行人之得，邑人之灾[4]。
九四：可贞，无咎[5]。
九五：无妄之疾，勿药有喜[6]。
上九：无妄行有眚，无攸利。

Translation：

The Unexpected：One should be steadfast and faithful if one starts with great success, otherwise one will suffer calamities. It is not auspicious to go anywhere.

Nine at the bottom line：Go with no expectation. Good fortune.

Six at the second line：Reap without sowing and have a cultivated field without opening up wastelands. It is favourable if one travels with a purpose.

Six at the third line：An unexpected disaster：a cow was tied here and then stolen by a passerby, which is a disaster for the town's people.

Nine at the fourth line：The matter can be anticipated by divination. No big trouble.

Nine at the fifth line：The unexpected disease will be naturally cured without need to take medicine.

Nine at the top line: It is disadvantageous to take action with no expectation. This leads to calamity.

Notes:

1. 无妄 (wu wang) is interpreted as wild fancy or trouble-maker by some scholars; and in the *I Ching on Silk* it is written as 无孟 (wu meng), meaning no reluctance. We extend it to denote 无望 (wu wang), do not expect or without hope.

2. 其匪正有眚 (qi fei zheng you sheng): calamity will befall one if one does not observe the principle of steadfast faithfulness. 匪 (fei): no, does not. 匪正 (fei zheng): deviate from the right path. 眚 (sheng): calamity, disaster.

3. 不耕获, 不菑畬 (bu geng huo, bu zi yu): reap without sowing and get cultivated fields without opening up wastelands. 菑 (zi): open up wasteland. 畬 (yu): cultivated or good land.

4. 无妄之灾, 或系之牛, 行人之得, 邑人之灾 (wu wang zhi zai, huo ji zhi niu, xing ren zhi de, yi ren zhi zai): unexpected disaster. A cow was tied here by someone and it was stolen by a passerby. The gain of the passerby is the disaster of the town's people. 邑 (yi): town.

5. 可贞, 无咎 (ke zhen, wu jiu): the matter can be predicted by divination. It shows no important trouble.

6. 无妄之疾, 勿药有喜 (wu wang zhi ji, wu yao you xi): the unexpected illness will be naturally cured without taking medicine. 疾 (ji): illness, disease. The ancient Chinese considered recovery from illness a joyous event.

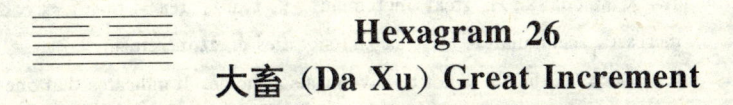

Hexagram 26
大畜 (Da Xu) Great Increment

The Chinese text:

大畜[1]：利贞。不家食[2]、吉。利涉大川。
初九：有厉，利已[3]。
九二：舆说輹[4]。
九三：良马逐，利艰贞[5]，日闲舆卫[6]，利有攸往。
六四：童牛之牿[7]，元吉。
六五：豮豕之牙[8]，吉。
上九：何天之衢[9]，亨。

Translation：

Great Increment：It is favourable to be steadfast and faithful. One does not have meals at home. Advantageous to cross great rivers.

Nine at the bottom line：One should cease action when faced with danger.

Nine at the second line：The wheel is off the carriage.

Nine at the third line：Good horses are chasing each other. Favourable if one keeps the principle of steadfast faithfuness. Practise every day defending with carriage and horse. It is advantageous to take a trip.

Six at the fourth line：Curb a bull by means of tying a horizontal stick to his horns. Good fortune from the beginning.

Six at the fifth line：Restrain a pig by binding it to a stake. Good luck.

Nine at the top line：Shoulder heaven's wide and level road and great success follows.

Notes：

1. 大畜(da xu)：great increment. 畜(xu)：rear, raise, save, increase, accumulate. 大畜(da xu) signifies great increment.

2. 不家食(bu jia shi)：not to have meals at home. It indicates that one can earn a livelihood by working for the monarch.

3. 有厉，利已(you li, li yi)：faced with danger, one ought to stop action. 厉(li)：danger. 已(yi)：cease, stop.

4. 輿说輹 (yu tuo fu): the body of the cart is apart from its wheel. 说 (tuo) is identical with 脱 (tuo), meaning separate, take off.

5. 良马逐，利艰贞 (liang ma zhu, li jian zhen): good horses are chasing one after another. It is advantageous to be steadfast and faithful in hard times. 逐 (zhu): chase, pursue, run.

6. 日闲舆卫 (ri xian yu wei): train horses and chariots every day for the purpose of defence. 闲 (xian): train, practise.

7. 童牛之牿 (tong niu zhi gu): tie a horizontal stick to the horns of a calf (if it should hurt people). 童牛 (tong niu): calf; young bull. 牿 (gu): a horizontal stick tied to the horns of a bull as a yoke to prevent it hurting people.

8. 豮豕之牙 (fen tun zhi ya): tie a small pig to a stake (lest it run away). 豮 (fen): little pig or young hog. 牙 (ya): stake used to hold pigs. Another interpretation of the phrase is that one castrates a pig so that it will not bite although it has teeth. This is not convincing.

9. 何天之衢 (he tian zhi qu): to shoulder heaven's wide and level road. 何 (he) is 荷 (he), meaning carry with the shoulder. 衢 (qu): wide and level road in the heavens.

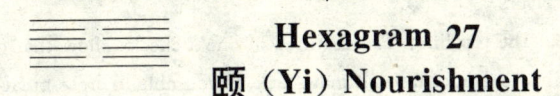

Hexagram 27
颐 (Yi) Nourishment

The Chinese text:

颐[1]：贞吉。观颐，自求口实[2]。
初九：舍尔灵龟，观我朵颐[3]，凶。
六二：颠颐，拂经，于丘颐，征凶[4]。
六三：拂颐、贞凶[5]，十年勿用，无攸利。

六四：颠颐，吉。虎视眈眈，其欲逐逐[6]，无咎。
六五：拂经，居贞，吉。不可涉大川。
上九：由颐，厉吉[7]，利涉大川。

Translation：

Nourishment：Good fortune. The features of one's cheeks tell that one can earn oneself a livelihood.

Nine at the bottom line：Ignore the omen indicated by your sacred tortoise and by only looking at my bulging cheeks. Misfortune.

Six at the second line：The shivering cheeks and the feature of one's neck and back as revealed when knocked on indicate that it is not fortunate to take military action.

Six at the third line：Cheeks knocked on, ill omen manifested. Do not do anything important for ten years. Disadvantageous.

Six at the fourth line：Shaking one's cheeks, Good omen occured. The two eyes are staring with courage as great as the tiger's. The face shows sincerity and honesty. No disaster.

Six at the fifth line：Knocking on one's neck and finding it auspicious for one to follow the principle of steadfast faithfulness. Do not ford great rivers.

Nine at the top line：The features of one's cheeks show that one will turn future danger into ultimate luck. Favourable to cross great rivers.

Notes

1. 颐 (yi)：literally means cheek. Its extended meaning is nourishment because food cannot nourish unless it is chewed in the mouth.

2. 观颐，自求口实 (guan yi, zi qiu kou shi)：to know whether or not one can earn a livelihood oneself by studying the features of one's cheeks. 观颐 (guanyi)：look at one's cheeks. 口食 (kou shi)：food in one's mouth. This hexagram appears to be a Zhou Dynasty record of

how to analyze physiognomy.

3. 舍尔灵龟，观我朵颐(she er ling gui, guan wo duo yi): ignore the omen shown in your tortoise shell and watch carefully my bulging cheeks. 舍(she): abandon, ignore. 尔(er): you, your. 灵龟(ling gui): holy tortoise. The ancient Chinese thought that a turtle was able to live a long life without eating anything, therefore took it as sacred. 朵颐(duo yi): bulging cheek.

4. 颠颐，拂经，于丘颐，征凶(dian yi, fu jing, yu qiu yi, zheng xiong): one's cheeks were found shivering and then one's neck and back were knocked on. The features indicate misfortune if military action is taken. 颠颐(dian yi): shivering cheek. 拂经(fu jing): to knock on one's neck and back (for the purpose of divination).

5. 拂颐、贞凶(fu yi, zhen xiong): knocking at one's cheeks, one finds signs of misfortune.

6. 虎视眈眈，其欲逐逐(hu shi dan dan, qi yu zhu zhu), one's eyes are staring hard and courageous as a tiger's eyes. One's face shows sincerity and honesty. 虎视眈眈(hu shi dan dan) describes courage and morale seen in one's eyes. 欲(yu) is written in the *I Ching on Silk as* 容(rong). We know from interpretation of the preceding lines that this hexagram is telling one's fortune by looking into one's face. Therefore 容, instead of 欲, is correct. 逐逐(zhu zhu): sincerity and honesty shown in the feature of one's face.

7. 由颐，厉吉(you yi, li ji): the appearance of one's cheeks shows that one may turn danger into luck.

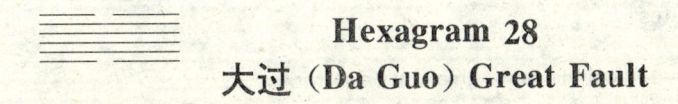

Hexagram 28
大过 (Da Guo) Great Fault

The Chinese text:

大过[1]：栋桡[2]，利有攸往，亨。
初六：藉用白茅[3]，无咎。
九二：枯杨生稊，老夫得其女妻[4]，无不利。
九三：栋桡，凶。
九四：栋隆，吉。有它吝[5]。
九五：枯杨生华，老妇得其士夫[6]，无咎，无誉。
上六：过涉灭顶[7]，凶，无咎。

Translation：

Great Fault：The ridgepole of the house is bent by a weight. It is favourable to take a trip. Great success.

Six at the bottom line：Cover the land with cogongrass (white grasses) in preparation for a sacrifice, which expresses one's piety. No disaster.

Nine at the second line：The withered willow sprouts and the old man takes a young wife. Nothing is unfavourable.

Nine at the third line：The ridgepole of the house is bent by weight. Misfortune.

Nine at the fourth line：The house ridgepole is bent upward. Good fortune, but an accident will happen.

Nine at the fifth line：The withered willow blooms and the old woman gets a young husband. Neither calamity nor glory comes about.

Six at the top line：(Ignorant of the depth of water), one is covered by water when fording a river. But no disaster takes place.

Notes：

1. 大过 (da guo)：great fault or error.
2. 栋桡 (dong rao)：the ridgepole and beam of a building are bent. The major beam of a house is named 栋 (dong), meaning ridgepole. 桡 (rao)：a kind of tree, describing the bent state of the ridgepole.

3. 藉用白茅(jie yong bai mao): cover a piece of land with cogongrass (for preparation for offerings) to manifest piety. 藉(jie): to pave or cover. 茅(mao): cogongrass, a white grass.

4. 枯杨生稊，老夫得其女妻(ku yang sheng di, lao fu de qi nu qi): the withered willow sprouts and the old man takes a young wife. 稊(di) is 稚(zhi), a bud sprouted from an old root.

5. 栋隆，吉．有它吝(dong long, ji, you tuo lin): the upwardly bent ridgepole of the house indicates good fortune. But beware of future accident. 隆(long): bent upward. 有它(you tuo): an accident will occur.

6. 枯杨生华，老妇得其士夫(ku yang sheng hua, lao fu de qi shi fu): the withered willow blooms and the old woman gets a young husband. 华(hua): blossom, flower. 士夫(shi fu): young husband.

7. 过涉灭顶(guo she mie ding): (not knowing the depth of the river), one is covered by water during one's crossing. 灭(mie): over, to cover. 顶(ding): head.

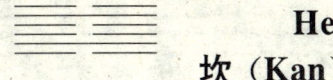

Hexagram 29
坎(Kan) Watery Danger

The Chinese text:

习坎[1]：有孚维心，亨，行有尚[2]。
初六：习坎，入于坎窞[3]，凶。
九二：坎有险，求小得[4]。
六三：来之坎，坎险且枕[5]。入于坎窞，勿用。
六四：樽酒，簋贰，用缶，纳约自牖[6]，终无咎。
九五：坎不盈，祗既平[7]，无咎。

61

上六：系用徽纆，寘于丛棘，三岁不得[8]，凶。

Trasnslation：

Watery Danger：Danger after danger. However, keeping sincerity in mind brings great success. One is rewarded for one's conduct.

Six at the bottom line：Danger after danger. One falls into a dangerous pit. Misfortune.

Nine at the second line：One should only seek small gains when faced with watery danger.

Six at the third line：One meets dangers when leaving and returning. One falls into a deep watery pit. Do not use this line.

Six at the fourth line：When offering sacrifice, one uses wine in the cup and grain in the bowl, and then fills the pot with wine by taking it with a spoon through a window. As a result, no calamity takes place.

Nine at the fifth line：The watery pit is not filled. Be calm and the danger will disappear naturally. No disaster.

Six at the top line：Bind a prisoner with black rope and put him into prison. This man will be in prison for three years. Misfortune.

Notes：

1. 坎(kan)：fall or danger. This hexagram is called 习坎(xi kan), that is, danger upon danger, because it is composed of two trigrams of Kan. 习(xi)：to be repeated. 坎(kan) is identical with 赣(gan) in classical Chinese. Hence it is written as 赣 in the *I Ching on Silk*.

2. 有孚维心，亨，行有尚(you fu wei xin, heng, xing you shang)：keep the principle of sincerity and faithfulness in mind. Succeed and be rewarded. 孚(fu)：sincerity and faithfulness. 维(wei)：in connection with, linked. 尚(shang)：reward.

3. 入于坎窞(ru yu kan dan)：fall into a dangerous pit. 窞(dan)：small pit or hole.

4. 坎有险，求小得(kan you xian, qiu xiao de)：danger is in the pit. Therefore, seek only small gains.

5. 来之坎，坎险且枕(lai zhi kan, kan xian qie zhen)：dangers found when going forth and returning. The water is dangerous and deep. 之(zhi)：go forth, leave. 枕(zhen)：deep.

6. 樽酒簋，贰用缶，纳约自牖(zun jiu gui, er yong fou, na yao zi you)：when offering sacrifice, one uses a cup of wine and a bowl of grain at first and then utilizes a pot which is filled with wine taken with a spoon through the window. 樽(zun)：wine utensil in ancient China. 簋(gui)：a container made of bamboo in ancient China. 贰(er)：secondary, additional. 约(yao)：wine spoon. 牖(you)：window.

7. 坎不盈，衹既平(kan bu ying, zhi ji ping)：The pit cannot be filled. Be calm and the danger will disappear naturally. 衹(zhi)：calm and peace; a different intepretation is hill.

8. 系用徽纆，寘于丛棘，三岁不得(ji yong hui mo, zhi yu cong ji, san sui bu de)：binded with a black rope, one was put into prison for three years. 系(ji)：bind, tie. 徽纆(hui mo)：black rope used to bind prisoners in ancient times. 寘(zhi)：put, place. 丛棘(cong ji)：thistles and thorns put outside the prison to restrain prisoners from escape. 三岁不得(san sui bu de)：to be in prison for three years.

Hexagram 30
离（Li）Fire

The Chinese text：

　　离[1]：利贞，亨。畜牝牛[2]，吉。
　　初九：履错然敬之[3]，无咎。

六二：黄离，元吉[4]。
九三：日昃之离[5]，不鼓缶而歌[6]，则大耋之嗟[7]，凶。
九四：突如其来如，焚如，死如，弃如[8]。
六五：出涕沱若，戚嗟若[9]，吉。
上九：王用出征，有嘉折首，获匪其丑[10]，无咎。

Translation：

Fire： It is advantageous to observe the principle of steadfast faithfulness. Great success. Raising a cow is auspicious.

Nine at the bottom line： One should show respect and piety as soon as one starts the ceremony. No harm.

Six at the second line： It is auspicious to trap birds and beasts with a yellow net.

Nine at the third line： It is misfortune to catch game at the setting sun, to sing without knocking on a pot for accompaniment or, if an old man sighs.

Nine at the fourth line： The undutiful son once driven out returns. He is burnt, killed and his body thrown away.

Six at the fifth line： One weeps with continuous tears like rain fall and one sighs with worry and sadness. Good fortune.

Nine at the top line： The king takes military action. He issues an edict and grants a reward to those who capture the leader of the enemy rather than the followers. No disaster.

Notes：

1. 离(li) is written as 罗(luo) in the *I Ching on Silk* and the two characters are identical in classical Chinese, meaning net, catch, trap or separate. 离(li) also shares the meaning of 丽(li), that is, addition, experience, bright.

2. 畜牝牛(xu pin niu)：rearing a cow. 畜：raise, rear. 牝：female.

3. 履错然敬之(lu cuo ran jing zhi) is written as 礼昔然敬之(li xi ran jing zhi) in the *I Ching on Silk*. 错(cuo)and 昔(xi)can be substituted for each other in classical Chinese, meaning initial, original, start or begin. According to the *I Ching on Silk*, this expression would better be interpreted as " one ought to show respect and piety from the start of one's practice of ceremony."

4. 黄离，元吉(huang li, yuan ji)：auspicious to catch game with a yellow net. 离(li) here means net. As mentioned in preceding hexagrams, yellow was considered a fortunate colour in the Shang and Zhou Dynasties.

5. 日昃之离(ri ze zhi li)：open the net to trap game in the light of the setting sun. 昃(ze)：sun after noon, that is, the setting sun.

6. 不鼓缶而歌(bu gu fou er ge)：sing without knocking on a pot for accompaniment. 缶(fou)：clay pot. 鼓(gu)：knock.

7. 大耋之嗟(da die zhi jie)：sigh of an aged man. 耋(die)：a general name for old man. 嗟(jie)：sigh.

8. 突如其来如，焚如，死如，弃如(tu ru qi lai ru, fen ru, si ru, qi ru)：on the undutiful son's return, he was burned, killed and thrown away. The action of driving out the undutiful son is called 突(tu) which is also written as 㐬. Being burnt, killed and cast away unburied were the punishments for an undutiful son in ancient China.

9. 出涕沱若，戚嗟若(chu ti tuo ruo, qi jie ruo)：shed tears as rain falls and deeply sigh with worry and sadness. 沱若(tuo ruo)：look like rain-fall. 戚(qi)：worry and sadness. 嗟(jie)：sigh.

10. 王用出征，有嘉折首，获匪其丑(wang yong chu zheng, you jia zhe shou, huo fei qi chou)：when taking military action, the king gives rewards to those who capture the leader of the enemy rather than his followers. 嘉(jia)：grant rewards. 折(zhe)：conquer, capture. 匪(fei)：no, not. 丑(chou)：friends or followers.

Part Two

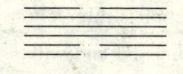

Hexagram 31
咸(Xian) Sensation

The Chinese text：

咸¹：亨，利贞。取女，吉²。
初六：咸其拇³。
六二：咸其腓⁴，凶。居吉。
九三：咸其股，执其随⁵，往吝。
九四：贞吉，悔亡。憧憧往来，朋从尔思⁶。
九五．咸其脢⁷，兀悔。
上六：咸其辅颊舌⁸。

Translation：

Sensation：One should be sincere and faithful when successful. It is auspicious to take a wife.

Six at the bottom line：One's toes are stirred by emotion.

Six at the second line：One's calves are stirred by feeling. Ill omen. It is auspicious if none of the family member leaves home.

Nine at third line：One's whole body moves as one's thighs are stirred by emotions. Trouble arises if one travels to a destination.

Nine at the fourth line：The divination shows good fortune and that regrets will disappear. You are wavering in determining whether or not to go, but your friends will follow your decision.

Nine at the fifth line：One's back is stirred by emotion. No regret.

Six at the top line：When speaking, one's jaw, face and tongue are trembling, stirred by emotion.

Notes:

1. 咸 (xian): sensation, feeling, affection, intercourse; here it represents the intimate relation between husband and wife.

2. 取女, 吉 (qu nu, ji): auspicious to marry a girl. 取 (qu) is 娶 (qu), to marry.

3. 咸其拇 (xian qi mu): one's toes are stirred by emotion. 拇 (mu): toe.

4. 咸其腓 (xian qi fei): one's calves are moved by feeling. 腓 (fei): calf of leg.

5. 咸其股, 执其随 (xian qi gu, zhi qi sui): one's body is in motion as one's thighs are stirred by emotion. 执 (zhi): hold, cause. 股 (gu): thigh.

6. 憧憧往来, 朋从尔思 (chong chong wang lai, peng cong er si): waver in determining whether to leave or not; your friends would prefer to follow your opinion. 憧憧 (chong chong): hard to decide, hesitation. 尔 (er): you, your.

7. 咸其脢 (xian qi mei): one's back is stirred by emotion. 脢 (mei): back.

8. 咸其辅颊舌 (xian qi fu jia she): one's jaws, tongue, face are trembling with emotion. 辅 (fu): jaw, gum. 颊 (jia): face.

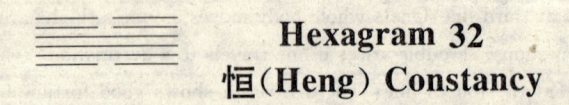

Hexagram 32
恒 (Heng) Constancy

The Chinese text:

恒¹: 亨, 无咎。利贞, 利有攸往。

初六：浚恒，贞凶[2]，无攸利。
九二：悔亡[3]。
九三：不恒其德，或承之羞，贞吝[4]。
九四：田无禽[5]。
六五：恒其德，贞妇人吉，夫子凶[6]。
上六：振恒[7]，凶。

Translation：

Constancy：Sublime success and no disasters. It is advantageous to follow the principle of faithfulness and take a trip.

Six at the bottom line：It is misfortune and unfavourable to seek something without stop.

Nine at the second line：One is free from regrets.

Nine at the third line：One who cannot keep moral principles steadfastly will endure humiliation. Misfortune.

Nine at the fourth line：There are no birds and beasts in the fields.

Six at the fifth line：Constantly act on moral principles. Good fortune for women and an ill omen for men.

Six at the top line：No good outcome arises if one seeks something ceaselessly.

Notes：

1. 恒(heng)：constant, permanent, eternal.
2. 浚恒，贞凶 (jun heng, zhen xiong)：the divination manifests misfortune for one who seeks something ceaselessly. In the *I Ching on Silk*，浚恒(jun heng) at the bottom line and 振恒(zhen heng) at the top line of this hexagram are both written as 复恒(qiong heng); and interpreted as 求 (qiu), to seek, which is in accord with the interpretation of the expression in 象 (Xiang), one of the ten *Appendixes to the I Ching*.

3. 悔亡(hui wang)：free from regret. 亡(wang)：disappear, free from.
4. 不恒其德，或承之羞，贞吝(bu heng qi de, huo cheng zhi xiu, zhen lin)：one suffers humiliation because one cannot constantly adhere to moral principles. Hard fortune. 承(cheng)：suffer, endure.
5. 田无禽(tian wu qin)：no birds and beasts in the fields.
6. 恒其德，贞妇人吉，夫子凶(heng qi de, zhen fu ren ji, fu zi xiong)：consistently stick to moral principles. Good fortune for a woman, and an ill omen for a man. 夫子(fu zi)：man.
7. 振恒(zhen heng)：seek something ceaselessly.

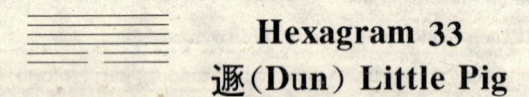

Hexagram 33
遯(Dun) Little Pig

The Chinese text：

遯[1]：亨小，利贞[2]。
初六：遯尾，厉[3]，勿用有攸往。
六二：执之用黄牛之革，莫之胜说[4]。
九三：系遯，有疾厉[5]，畜臣妾[6]，吉。
九四：好遯，君子吉，小人否[7]。
九五：嘉遯，贞吉[8]。
上九：肥遯[9]，无不利。

Translation：

Little Pig：One should consult an oracle when having a little success.
Six at the bottom line：Do not go anywhere for your pig's tail is in danger of being cut off.

Six at the second line: The little pig tied with yellow ox leather cannot escape.

Nine at the third line: A little pig is ill and in dangerous condition for being tied. It is auspicious to raise slaves.

Nine at the fourth line: A little pig is lovely, which is auspicious for a superior man, not an ordinary person.

Nine at the fifth line: A little pig is praised. Good fortune.

Nine at the top line: A little pig has grown fat (enough to be used as a sacrifice). Nothing is unfavourable.

Notes:

1. 遯(dun) is also written as 逐 or 遁(dun) and in the *I Ching on Silk* as 掾. These two are in general interpreted as escape or seclude. However, following Professor Gao Heng's convincing research, we take this character to mean a little pig, which occurs frequently in this hexagram.

2. 亨小, 利贞(heng xiao, li zhen): a little success. Thus one should consult an oracle.

3. 遯尾, 厉(dun wei, li): a pig is faced with a danger of having its tail cut off.

4. 执之用黄牛之革, 莫之胜说(zhi zhi yong huang niu zhi ge, mo zhi sheng tuo): tie a pig with yellow ox leather and it cannot escape. 执(zhi): hold, tie, bind. 革(ge): leather. 说(tuo): escape.

5. 系遯, 有危厉(ji dun, you wei li): a little pig is ill and in dangerous condition because it is tied.

6. 畜臣妾(xu chen qie): have and raise man and woman slaves. 臣(chen): male slave. 妾(qie): female slaves.

7. 好遯, 君子吉, 小人否(hao dun, jun zi ji, xiao ren pi): a little pig is lovely. Propitious for superior men but not for common folks.

8. 嘉遯, 贞吉(jia dun, zhen ji): a little pig is praised. Good fortune. 嘉(jia): praise, admire.

9. 肥遯 (fei dun): a little pig becomes fat, (thus it can be used as a sacrifice).

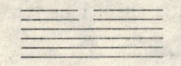

Hexagram 34
大壯 (Da Zhuang) Great Power

The Chinese text:

大壯：利貞[1]。
初九：壯于趾，征凶，有孚[2]。
九二：貞吉。
九三：小人用壯，君子用罔[3]，貞厲。羝羊觸藩，羸其角[4]。
九四：貞吉，悔亡。藩決不羸，壯于大輿之輹。
六五：喪羊于易[6]，无悔。
上六：羝羊觸藩，不能退，不能遂[7]，无攸利。艱則吉。

Translation:

Great Power: It is advantageous to remain steadfast and faithful.

Nine at the bottom line: Taking military action with injured feet, one meets misfortune, but one is still faithful.

Nine at the second line: Be steadily faithful. Good fortune.

Nine at the third line: An ordinary person is proud of his great power while a superior man treats everything in a natural way. Ill omen. Butting against a fence, a ram's horns are snared by thick ropes.

Nine at the fourth line: It is auspicious to be steadfastly faithful. Regrets disappear. Freed from the ropes, the ram breaks the fence and also damages the wheel of a cart.

Six at the fifth line: The ram is missing in the grain ground. Do not regret.

Six at the top line: The ram becomes entangled when butting the fence. It can neither move forward nor retreat. Nothing is favourable. One cannot meet good fortune until hard times pass.

Notes:

1. 大壮(da zhuang): great righteousness, greatness, progress or injury.

2. 壮于趾,征凶,有孚(zhuang yu zhi, zheng xiong, you fu): misfortune to take military action with injured toes. But one is still faithful. 壮(zhuang): injure, wound. 趾(zhi): toes; in the *I Ching on Silk* it is written as 止(zhi).

3. 小人用壮,君子用罔(xiao ren yong zhuan, jun zi yong wang): an ordinary person is proud of his power whereas a superior man treats everything naturally. 壮(zhuang): greatness, power. 罔(wang): Taoist " nothing "; meaning " treat everything naturally."

4. 羝羊触藩,羸其角(di yang chu fan, lei qi jiao): butting against the fence, a ram's horns are snared. 羝羊(di yang): ram. 藩(fan): fence. 羸(lei): thick rope or to entangle.

5. 藩决不羸,壮于大舆之輹(fan jue bu lei, zhuang yu da yu zhi fu): the fence is broken by the ram free from the entanglement of ropes and the ram also damages the wheel of the cart. 壮(zhuang): damage, injure. 舆(yu): cart, carriage. 輹(fu): spoke of wheel.

6. 丧羊于易(sang yang yu yi): the ram is missing in the grain ground. 易(yi) means change in general, but in this special case it denotes an area used by farmers to dry grain.

7. 羝羊触藩,不能退,不能遂(di yang chu fan, bu neng tui, bu neng sui): butting against the fence, the ram becomes entangled. It can neither advance nor retreat. 遂(sui): advance.

Hexagram 35
晋（Jin）Advance

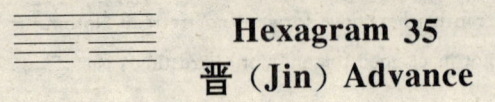

The Chinese text：

晋¹：康侯用锡马蕃庶²，昼日三接³。
初六：晋如、摧如，贞吉⁴。罔孚，裕无咎⁵。
六二：晋如愁如，贞吉⁶。受兹介福于其王母⁷。
六三：众允，悔亡⁸。
九四：晋如鼫鼠⁹，贞厉。
六五：悔亡，失得勿恤¹⁰，往吉，无不利。
上九：晋其角，维用伐邑¹¹，厉吉，无咎，贞吝。

Translation：

Advance：Marquis Kang has a great number of horses bequeathed by the King and they meet thrice a day.

Nine at the bottom line：One's advance is frustrated. It is favourable to remain steadily faithful. This man is not sincere and faithful. He must treat people leniently in order to avoid disaster.

Six at second line：Advance gloomily. Auspicious if one is faithful. One is greatly blessed by one's grandmother.

Six at the third line：Trusted by the multitude, one's regrets disappear.

Nine at the fourth line：Advance like a big rat. Misfortune.

Six at the fifth line：One will certainly gain as the regrets disappear. Do not worry. It is favourable to go and everything is advantageous.

Nine at the top line：The spearhead advances to conquer the city. It is fortunate although there are dangers. No disaster but some difficulties.

Notes:

1. 晋(jin)：advance, promotion. It is written as 溍 in *the I Ching on Silk*.

2. 康侯用锡马蕃庶(kang hou yong xi ma fan shu)：Marquis Kang has a great number of horses bequeathed by the King. 康侯(kang hou)：the Marquis of An Kang or a brother of King Wu in Zhou Dynasty. The former seems more convincing. 锡(xi)：bequeath, grant, give. 蕃庶(fan shu)：reproduce；here means many, great number.

3. 昼日三接(zhou ri san jie)：being interviewed thrice a day.

4. 晋如摧如，贞吉(jin ru cui ru, zhen ji)：the advance is frustrated. Propitious to be staunchly faithful. 晋(jin)：advance. 摧(cui)：frustrated, blocked, damaged.

5. 罔孚，裕无咎(wang fu, yu wu jiu)：No faithfulness. Treating people leniently can avoid disaster. 罔(wang)：without, nothing. 裕(yu)：lenient, mild.

6. 晋如愁如，贞吉(jin ru chou ru, zhen ji)：advance with gloomy feeling. Fortunate to remain faithful.

7. 受兹介福于其王母(shou zi jie fu yu qi wang mu)：greatly blessed by one's grandmother. 兹(zi)：here. 介(jie)：great. 王母(wang mu)：grandmother.

8. 众允，悔亡(zhong yun, hui wang)：trusted by the multitude, one's regrets disappear. 允(yun)：trust. 亡(wang)：disappear, escape.

9. 晋如鼫鼠(jin ru shi shu)：advancing like a big rat. According to Professor Gao Heng, 如(ru) here means similar to. 鼫鼠(shi shu)：big rat.

10. 悔亡，失得勿恤(hui wang, shi de wu xu)：one must have a gain as regrets disappear. Do not worry. 失(shi) is written as 矢(shi)in the *I Ching on Silk*, meaning certainly. 恤(xu)：worry.

11. 晋其角，维用伐邑(jin qi jiao, wei yong fa yi)：the spearhead advances to subdue the city. 邑(yi)：city.

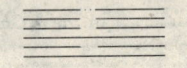

Hexagram 36
明夷(Ming Yi) Darkness

The Chinese text:

明夷[1]：利艰贞。
初九：明夷于飞，垂其翼[2]；君子于行，三日不食[3]。有攸往，主人有言[4]。
六二：明夷，夷于左股，用拯马壮[5]，吉。
九三：明夷于南狩，得其大首，不可疾贞[6]。
六四：入于左腹，获明夷之心，于出门庭[7]。
六五：箕子之明夷[8]，利贞。
上六：不明晦，初登于天，后入于地[9]。

Translation:

Darkness: It will be beneficial if one follows the principle of steadfast faithfulness in hardship.

Nine at the bottom line: The sacred bird Ming Yi flew with drooping wings. A superior man had no food to eat for three days when travelling away. He is blamed by his master although he has taken a journey.

Six at the second line: One's leg is injured. A strong horse is needed to save one from danger. Good luck results.

Nine at the third line: Hunting in the outskirts when the solar eclipse occurs, one gains a fine horse with four white hooves. Do not hurry to train and use it.

Six at the fourth line: One caught Ming Yi, the legendary bird, and took its heart and then carried it out of one's home in a ritual way.

Six at the fifth line: It was favourable for Qi Zi to remain steadily faithful when the eclipse occured.

Six at the top line: When the solar eclipse took place the sky was unclear and dark. The sun rose to the heavens first and then dropped to the ground.

Notes:

1. 明夷(ming yi): darkness of the light; eclipse. 夷(yi) in this phrase is identical with 痍(yi), meaning injure, wound.
2. 明夷于飞，垂其翼(ming yi yu fei, chui qi yi): when flying, the bird Ming Yi lowers its wings. Considering the similar description in the *I Ching on Silk*, 明夷(ming yi) here obviously denotes a legendary bird.
3. 君子于行，三日不食(jun zi yu xing, san ri bu shi): the superior man had no food to eat for three days when he traveled.
4. 主人有言(zhu ren you yan): blamed by one's host. 言(yan): blame, complain.
5. 明夷，夷于左股，用拯马壮(ming yi, yi yu zuo gu, yong zheng ma zhuang): one's left leg was wounded when the solar eclipse occured. To save one, a strong horse was needed. 夷(yi): injure, wound. 股(gu): leg. A different interpretation of it is 般(ban), joint. 拯(zhen): save; it is written in the *I Ching on Silk as* 撜 which is also identical with 拼.
6. 明夷于南狩，得其大首，不可疾贞(ming yi yu nan shou, de qi da shou, bu ke ji zhen): an eclipse occurs when one hunts in the south. As a result, one captures a fine horse with four white hooves. However, do not hurry to train and use it. 于(yu): in or at (some place). 狩(shou): hunt by means of driving game with burning grasses. 首(shou): horse with four white hooves. 疾(ji): hurry, rash. This hexagram seems to describe the way to ward off disasters in ancient China when a solar eclipse took place.
7. 入于左腹，获明夷之心，于出门庭(ru yu zuo fu, huo ming yi zhi

79

xin, yu chu men ting): the legendary bird Ming Yi entered on the left side of one's stomach. In this way one obtained its heart and then rituxly carried the bird's heart outside one's gate. This line of the hexagram is also regarded as a description of how to keep calamities away in ancient times; a variety of interpretations are available.

8. 箕子之明夷(qi zi zhi ming yi): Qi Zi was there when an eclipse occured. 箕子(qi zi): a well-known high-ranking official who served King Zhou, the last king of the Shang Dynasty.

9. 不明晦, 初登于天, 后入于地(bu ming hui, chu deng yu tian, hou ru yu di): (when the solar eclipse took place) the sky became dark; the sun rose to the heavens at first and then fell to the gound. 晦 (hui):not bright, dark. 登(deng) rise.

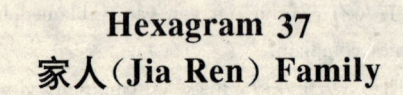

Hexagram 37
家人(Jia Ren) Family

The Chinese text:

家人¹：利女贞²。

初九：闲有家³，悔亡。

六二：无攸遂，在中馈⁴，贞吉。

九三：家人嗃嗃⁵，悔厉，吉。妇子嘻嘻⁶，终吝。

六四：富家，大吉⁷。

九五：王假有家，勿恤⁸，吉。

上九：有孚威如⁹，终吉。

Translation:

Family: It is appropriate for women of a family to practise the principle of steadfast faithfulness.

Nine at the bottom line: Home is guarded cautiously and regrettable events disappear.

Six at the second line: The women of a family serve meals at home without aspirations. Good fortune is assured.

Nine at the third line: If the family members are harshly reproached from time to time, good fortune will come ultimately although regrets and conflicts occur sometimes. But if the women and childen of the family treat one another in a unserious way, it will result in hardship in the end.

Six at the fourth line: The greatest fortune for a family is to make the household rich.

Nine at the fifth line: It is fortunate if a king drops in on one's family. No cause for worry.

Nine at the top line: Sincerity, faithfulness and authority in a family bring good luck ultimately.

Notes:

1. 家人(jia ren): a family. The interpretation of this hexagram is the earliest material reflecting the relationship between family members in ancient China.

2. 利女贞(li nu zhen): advantageous for women to be steadfast and faithful. 贞(zhen): steadfast and faithful.

3. 闲有家(xian you jia): the family takes precautions to guard the home. 闲(xian): guard, protect; it is also interpreted as practise by some scholars.

4. 无攸遂, 在中馈(wu you sui, zai zhong kui): women have no ambition but preparing meals for their family. 遂(sui): purpose, aim, desire, ambition. 馈(kui): to serve preople by making meal. 中馈(zhong kui): do service at home.

5. 家人嗃嗃(jia ren he he): the family members are sharply

reproached frequently. 嗃嗃 (he he): the sound of sharp reproach; describing the strict displine within a family.

6. 妇子嘻嘻 (fu zi xi xi): women and chidren laughs all day long. These words signify the disorder of a family. 嘻嘻 (xi xi): appearance of tittering and laughing.

7. 富家，大吉 (fu jia, da ji): to make a houshold wealthy is the greatest fortune.

8. 王假有家，勿恤 (wang ge you jia, wu xu): the king drops in on one's home. Do not worry about it. 假 (ge): arrive, come to; it is written in the *I Ching on Silk* as 叚, indentical to 假 in significance.

9. 有孚威如 (you fu wei ru): one has sincerity and authority in the family.

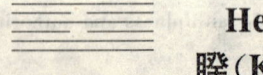

Hexagram 38
睽 (Kui) Conflict

The Chinese text:

睽[1]：小事吉。
初九：悔亡。丧马勿逐，自复，见恶人，无咎[2]。
九二：遇主于巷[3]，无咎。
六三：见舆曳，其牛掣[4]，其人天且劓[5]。无初，有终[6]。
九四：睽孤遇元夫，交孚[7]，厉，无咎。
六五：悔亡。厥宗噬肤，往何咎[8]。
上九：睽孤见豕负涂，载鬼一车[9]。先张之弧，后说之弧[10]，匪寇婚媾。往遇雨则吉。

Translation:

Conflict: One is fortunate in small matters.

Nine at the bottom line: Regrets vanish. The missing horses will return by themselves, therefore no need to look for them. No disaster happens when meeting with an evil person.

Nine at the second line: It is harmless if one encounters one's lord in a lane.

Six at the third line: The ox held up its horns when seeing the cart dragged. The driver of the cart is punished by having his face tatooed and nose cut off. He ends well although he suffers much pain earlier.

Nine at the fourth line: While isolated and lonely, one meets a good man who becomes one's faithful friend. No calamities arise but some dangers.

Six at the fifth line: Regret disappears. What disaster will befall if one goes to eat meat with members of one's own clan?

Nine at the top line: One sees a pig in the mud and a carriage full of demons when one is estranged and lonely. One shoots arrows first and then turns to a happy celebration with a pot of wine. One was not a robber but a wife-seeker. It is auspicious when one is caught in the rain on one's way.

Notes:

1. 睽(kui): originally meant that eyes turn away from each other; the extended meaning is breach, disagreeable, conflicting; 乖 (guai), perverse, is its subsitute in the *I Ching on Silk*.

2. 丧马勿逐，自复。见恶人，无咎(sang ma wu zhu, zi fu. jian e ren, wu jiu): do not look for the missing horses for they will certainly return by themselves. No harm is brought about when encountering an evil person. 逐(zhu): pursue, look for; it is replaced by its synonym 遂(sui) in the *I Ching on Silk*. 恶(e) is written as 亚(ya) in the *I Ching on Silk*, meaning evil.

3. 遇主于巷(yu zhu yu xiang): meeting with one's lord in a lane. 巷 (xiang): lane.

4. 见舆曳，其牛掣(jian yu ye, qi niu che)：the ox held up its horns when seeing the cart dragged. 舆(yu)：cart, carriage. 曳(ye)：drag, draw. 掣(che)：set horn upright; synonymous with 觢.

5. 其人天且劓(qi ren tian qie yi)：the cart driver suffered the penalties of tatooing the face and cutting the nose. 天(tian)：have the prisoner's face tatooed as a punishment for his crime; it was also called 墨刑(mo xing) in Zhou Dynasty. 劓(yi)：cut off one's nose.

6. 无初，有终(wu chu, you zhong)：good outcome arises though unfavourable at the beginning. 无初(wu chu)：one was punished and got no favour at the beginning.

7. 睽孤遇元夫，交孚(kui gu yu yuan fu, jiao fu)：while estranged and lonely, one meets a benevolent man with whom one shares faithful friendship. 元夫(yuan fu)：good man, benevolent person. 孚(fu)：sincere and faithful.

8. 厥宗噬肤，往何咎(jue zong shi fu, wang he jiu)：go there and eat meat with the people of one's own clan. What is wrong with it? 厥(jue)：one, someone. 噬(shi)：eat, bite. 肤(fu)：soft meat.

9. 睽孤见豕负涂，载鬼一车(kui gu jian shi fu tu, zai gui yi che)：one sees a pig with a muddy back and a carriage of ghosts when one is isolated and lonely. 豕(shi)：swine, pig. 涂(tu)：mud and earth.

10. 先张之弧，后说之弧(xian zhang zhi hu, hou yue zhi hu)：one shoots arrows first and then has a joyful celebration with a kettle of wine. In this expression, according to the *I Ching on Silk*, the first 弧(hu) denotes a bow and the second means a wine kettle. 说(yue)：joyful, pleased, happy.

Hexagram 39
蹇(Jian) Trouble

The Chinese text：

蹇[1]：利西南，不利東北[2]。利見大人，貞吉。
初六：往蹇，來譽[3]。
六二：王臣蹇蹇，匪躬之故[4]。
九三：往蹇，來反[5]。
六四：往蹇，來連[6]。
九五：大蹇，朋來[7]。
上六：往蹇，來碩[8]，吉。利見大人。

Translation：

Trouble: It is favourable to go to the southwest and unfavourable to go to the northeast. Auspicious to meet a great man.

Six at the bottom line: One encounters dangers and difficulties when one is away, but one returns with much glory.

Six at the second line: The King's ministers go through trouble after trouble not for their own sake.

Nine at the third line: One would better return when one runs into trouble and danger.

Six at the fourth line: Whether going or returning, one is always accompanied by difficulties.

Nine at the fifth line: Friends arrive and help when one meets with severe trouble.

Six at the top line: Go away in hardship but come back easily and leisurely. Good fortune. It is advantageous to see a great man.

Notes：

1. 蹇 (jian): originally meant lame and came to signify trouble or difficulty.

2. 利西南，不利東北 (li xi nan, bu li dong bei): favourable to go to southwest and unfavourable to northeast. Ancient Chinese thought so because the new moon rises in the southwest and disappears in the

northeast.

3. 往蹇，来誉(wang jian, lai yu)：go with risks and in difficulties but return with glory.

4. 王臣蹇蹇，匪躬之故(wang chen jian jian, fei gong zhi gu)：the King's ministers have undergone all sort of difficulties not for their own sake. 匪(fei)：not. 躬(gong)：self, oneself.

5. 往蹇，来反(wang jian, lai fan)：turn back if troubles are on one's trip. 反(fan)：return; identical with 返(fan) in this case.

6. 往蹇，来连(wang jian, lai lian)：going forth in troubles and returning in troubles, too. 连(lian) here is simalar to 辇(nian), dangers and difficulties.

7. 大蹇，朋来(da jian, peng lai)：friends arrive and offer help when one is in severe trouble.

8. 往蹇，来硕(wang jian, lai shuo)：leave under difficulties but return leisurely. 硕(shuo)：great; but here it means leisurely, easily.

Hexagram 40
解(Jie) Release

The Chinese text：

解[1]：利西南。无所往，其来复，吉。有攸往，夙吉[2]。

初六：无咎。

九二：田获三狐，得黄矢[3]，贞吉。

六三：负且乘，致寇至[4]，贞吝。

九四：解而拇，朋至斯孚[5]。

六五：君子维有解[6]，吉。有孚于小人[7]。

上六：公用射隼于高墉之上[8]，获之，无不利。

Translation:

Release: The south is advantageous. If there is no where to go, one has to go back to the original place.
Six at the bottom line: No calamities.
Nine at the second line: One gets three foxes and finds a golden arrow during one's hunting. The divinaton shows good fortune.
Six at the third line: Riding on a cart with a load on one's shoulder, one attracts robbers (and is robbed). A troublesome omen.
Nine at the fourth line: your friends do not believe you until you show your thumbs and toes.
Six at the fifth line: It is auspicious if a superior man is tied and then released. One is trusted by a lesser man.
Six at the top line: The princes and dukes shoot arrows at a hawk from atop a city wall and hit it. Nothing is disadvantageous.

Notes:

1. 解(jie): originally meant a sacred beast and its extended meaning is to release, loose.
2. 有攸往，夙吉(you you wang, su ji): take a trip and have early luck. 夙(su): early.
3. 田获三狐，得黄矢(tian huo san hu, de huang shi): one traps three foxes and finds a golden arrow while on one's hunt. 田(tian): hunt. 黄矢(huang shi): a golden arrow.
4. 负且乘，致寇至(fu qie cheng, zhi kou zhi): riding on a cart with a load on one's shoulder, one attracts robbers. 负(fu): to shoulder something.
5. 解而拇，朋至斯孚(jie er mu, peng zhi si fu): your friends do not believe you till you release your thumbs and toes. 拇(mu) denotes thumb and toe in classical Chinese.

6. 君子維有解 (jun zi wei you jie): a superior man is bound and then released. 維 (wei) is subsituted in the *I Ching on Silk* by 唯 (wei), meaning tie or bind.

7. 有孚于小人 (you fu yu xiao ren): being trusted by a mean fellow.

8. 公用射隼于高墉之上 (gong yong she sun yu gao yong zhi shang): the prince and dukes shoot arrows at an hawk from the top of a high city wall. 公 (gong): duke. Ancient Chinese noblemen were divided into the following five categories: duke, marquis, earl, viscount and baron. 隼 (sun): a bird in the eagle family. 墉 (yong): city wall.

Hexagram 41
损 (Sun) Loss

The Chinese text:

损[1]：有孚，元吉，无咎，可贞，利有攸往。曷之用？二簋可用享[2]。
初九：巳事遄往，无咎；酌损之[3]。
九二：利贞，征凶，弗损，益之[4]。
六三：三人行则损一人，一人行则得其友[5]。
六四：损其疾，使遄有喜[6]，无咎。
六五：或益之十朋之龟，弗克违[7]，元吉。
上九：弗损益之，无咎，贞吉，利有攸往。得臣无家[8]。

Translation:

Loss: Being sincere and faithful, one starts with good fortune and avoids disaster. It is advantageous to follow the principle of faithfulness and take a trip with a clear aim. What should be used as sacrifices for the gods and demons? Two bowls of food are alright.

Nine at the bottom line: There will be no danger if one hurries away to treat one's illness. However he ought to be thrifty in expenses.

Nine at the second line: Favourable to remain steadfast and faithful and disadvantageous to take military action. Do not decrease but increase.

Six at the third line: One person leaves because of disagreement when three men travel together. But a man may gain a friend as a companion if he travels alone at first.

Six at the fourth line: No way to have good luck and avert disaster unless one promptly recovers from one's disease.

Six at the fifth line: If given a fine turtle as valuable as ten pengs, one should not refuse it. Good fortune at the beginning.

Nine at the top line: Not to decrease but to increase. No harm. The divination shows good omen and that one can take a trip. When the King is helped by a good and able minister he forgets about his own home.

Notes:

1. 损(sun): lose, decrease.
2. 曷之用？二簋可用享(he zhi yong? er gui ke yong xiang): what should be used? Two bowls of food can be offered to the gods and demons. 曷(he): what. A different interpretation is 遏(e), signifying stop. 簋(gui): an ancient square grain container. 享(xiang): offer sacrifice to gods and demons.
3. 巳事遄往，无咎；酌损之(si shi chuan wang, wu jiu; zhuo sun zhi): hurrying away to treat one's illness brings no disaster, but the expenses ought to be limited. 巳(si): stop disease; here it means to treat one's illness in a hurry. Another interpretation is offering sacrifice. 遄(chuan): hurry, haste, prompt. It is written as 端(duan) in the *I Ching on Silk*, its synonym in classical Chinese.
4. 弗损，益之(fu sun, yi zhi): not to decrease but to increase. 弗

(fu): no, not.

5. 三人行则损一人，一人行则得其友 (san ren xing ze sun yi ren, yi ren xing ze de qi you): three men travel together and one leaves because of disagreement. However, if one person takes a journey, one may find a friend (as a companion).

6. 损其疾，使遄有喜 (sun qi ji, shi chuan you xi): there will be no luck unless one treats one's illness promptly. 疾 (ji): illness, disease. 使 (shi): thing or event. The character is replaced in the *I Ching on Silk* by 事 (shi), thing. This sentence is apparently a response to the first line of the same hexagram.

7. 或益之十朋之龟，弗克违 (huo yi zhi shi peng zhi gui, fu ke wei): perhaps one is given a tortoise as valuable as ten pengs, in this case, one cannot refuse it. 或 (huo): perhaps. 益 (yi): increase, add, gain. 十朋之龟 (shi peng zhi gui): a treasured tortoise worth ten pengs. 朋 (peng): money unit in ancient China; one peng is said to be equal to two shells (a different opinion is ten shells). The tortoise shell was used in ancient China as a money unit as well as an instrument for divination.

8. 得臣无家 (de chen wu jia): the King forgets about his home when helped by a good and able minister. 臣 (chen): good and able high officials.

Hexagram 42
益 (Yi) Gain

The Chinese text:

益[1]：利有攸往，利涉大川。

初九：利用为大作², 元吉, 无咎。
六二：或益之十朋之龟, 弗克违³, 永贞吉⁴。王用享于帝⁵, 吉。
六三：益之用凶事⁶, 无咎。有孚中行告公用圭⁷。
六四：中行告公从, 利用为依迁国⁸。
九五：有孚惠心, 勿问元吉⁹, 有孚惠我德¹⁰。
上九：莫益之, 或击之, 立心勿恒¹¹, 凶。

Translation:

Gain: It is favourable to take a trip and ford great rivers.

Nine at the bottom line: Appropriate to plough and sow. Auspicious and harmless from the beginning.

Six at the second line: If given a precious tortoise worth ten peng of shells, one should not refuse it. It is auspicious for one to be steadily faithful. Good fortune if the king offers the tortoise to the heavenly god.

Six at the third line: one practises the principle of increment upon misfortune. No disaster. (when calamities takes place), one ought to be sincere and faithful and report the message to the duke with a jade tablet by walking on the middle path.

Six at the fourth line: Walking on the middle path, one informs the duke of the emergency news to the duke and gains his recognition and support. Thus one will implement one's plan to move the whole country.

Nine at the fifth line: One is unquestionabaly successful from the start if sincere, faithful and humane. The person who is faithful and benefits me will certainly gain something.

Nine at the top line: One is not benefited and is attacked by others because of one's inconstant mind. Ill omen.

Notes:

1. 益(yi): increase, gain, abundance.

2. 利用为大作(li yong wei da zuo): advantageous to plant. 大作(da zuo): great thing, meaning to plough and sow.

3. 或益之十朋之龟,弗克违(huo yi zhi shi peng zhi gui, fu ke wei): when given a tortois as valuable as ten pengs one should not refuse it.

4. 永贞吉(yong zhen ji): auspicious to be always faithful. 永(yong): always, eternal.

5. 王用享于帝(wang yong xiang yu di): the king makes an offering to the heavenly god. 享(xiang): offer sacrifice.

6. 益之用凶事(yi zhi yong xiong shi): increase offered at disaster. 凶事(xiong shi): famine, war, diseases, etc..

7. 有孚中行,告公用圭(you fu zhong xing gao gong yong gui): practise the principle of the middle way with sincerity and faithfulness and use a jade tablet for sending a message. 孚(fu): sincere and faithful. 圭(gui): a square jade tablet used by messengers in ancient China to inform of urgent news.

8. 中行告公从,利用为依迁国(zhong xing gao gong cong, li yong wei yi qian guo): by walking on the middle path, one tells the news to the duke and he recognizes it. With the help of this recognition, one will fulfil his great mission to move the country. 从(cong): recognition or support. 为依迁国(wei yi qian guo): move a country. In ancient times, the whole of a country migrated in order to avoid war or great disaster. 依(yi) is written as 家(jia), clan, in the *I Ching on Silk*.

9. 有孚惠心,勿问元吉(you fu hui xin, wu wen yuan ji): a person with a sincere, faithful, humane heart and a mild personality unquestionabaly succeeds from the start.

10. 有孚惠我德(you fu hui wo de): if sincere and faithful, one must benefit from it. 德(de): benefit, gain.

11. 莫益之,或击之,立心勿恒(mo yi zhi, huo ji zhi, li xin wu heng): one is not benefited but attacked by somebody for his inconstancy of heart. 莫(mo): not, cannot. 或(huo): someone. 恒(heng): constant, permenant.

Hexagram 43
夬(Guai) Resolution

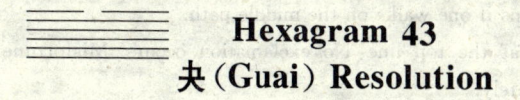

The Chinese text:

夬¹：扬于王庭，孚号有厉²。告自邑，不利即戎³，利有攸往。
初九：壮于前趾，往不胜⁴，为咎。
九二：惕号，莫夜有戎⁵，勿恤。
九三：壮于頄⁶，有凶。君子夬夬⁷，独行遇雨若濡，有愠⁸，无咎。
九四：臀无肤，其行次且⁹。牵羊悔亡，闻言不信¹⁰。
九五：苋陆夬夬¹¹。中行无咎。
上六：无号，终有凶¹²。

Translation:

Resolution: One makes a proclamation at the court of the king and straightfowardly points out the future danger. One also warns the people of the city that it is unfavourable to fight. Advantageous to take a trip.

Nine at the bottom line: To go with injured toes one cannot win. Disaster will follow.

Nine at the second line: One cries loudly about the enemy's action in the evening. But there is no need to worry about it.

Nine at the third line: One's face is injured. Misfortune. The superior man leaves with no hesitation. He is angry for being caught in the rain and getting wet. But no calamity will occur.

Nine at the fourth line: One acts in hardship because one's haunches have been flayed. To go and drag a sheep will lead to disappearance of regrets; but the listener does not believe it.

Nine at the fifth line: The goat leaves in determination. No trouble happens if one walks on the middle path.

Nine at the top line: No exclamation occurs. Misfortune will arise ultimately.

Notes:

1. 夬(guai): resolute, decision.
2. 扬于王庭，孚号有厉(yang yu wang ting, fu hao you li): make a proclaimation at the court of the king, reviel the alarming dangers staightforwardly. 扬(yang): proclaim, declare.
3. 告自邑，不利即戎(gao zi yi, bu li ji rong): admornish the people in one's own city not to fight immediately. 邑(yi): city. 戎(rong): army. Here it means to fight with an army.
4. 壮于前趾，往不胜(zhuang yu qian zhi, wang bu sheng): toes injured, one cannot win when one comes to fight. 壮(zhuang): injure, wound.
5. 惕号，莫夜有戎(ti hao, mo ye you rong): cry out loudly with fear when military danger occurs in the evening. 惕(ti): fear. 莫(mo): darkness, evening.
6. 壮于頄(zhuang yu kui): injoury in the face. 頄(kui): face, cheek.
7. 君子夬夬(jun zi guai guai): the superior man left with resolution. 夬夬(guai guai): describing the feature of one's leaving with firm determination. They are also interpreted as 趹, rapid walk. In the *I Ching on Silk* it is written as 缺(que), meaning to leave.
8. 独行遇雨若濡，有愠(du xing yu yu ruo ru, you yun): one is angry about being caught in the rain and getting wet when walking alone. 若(ruo): and. 濡(ru): wet. 愠(yun): angry, hate.
9. 臀无肤，其行次且(tun wu fu, qi xing ci qie): moving with difficulties because one's haunches have been flayed. 次且(ci qie) is identical with 趑趄, meaning unconvenient action.

10. 牵羊悔亡，闻言不信(qian yang hui wang, wen yan bu xin): no regret if one drags a sheep. But one does not believe so. 悔亡(hui wang): regrets vanish.

11. 苋陆夬夬(xian lu guai guai): a goat walks determinedly without stop. 苋(xian) was understood as a Chinese herb medicine or animal skin or 莞(guan), a plant like an onion. However, it was often interpreted by scholars in the Yuan and Ming Dynasties as goat, which we agree with. 陆(lu): harmony.

12. 无号，终有凶(wu hao, zhong you xiong): no exclamation; disaster arises in the end.

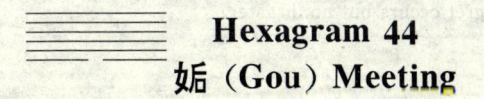

Hexagram 44
姤（Gou）Meeting

The Chinese text:

姤[1]：女壮，勿用取女[2]。
初六：系于金柅[3]，贞吉。有攸往，见凶。羸豕孚蹢躅[4]。
九二：包有鱼，无咎。不利宾[5]。
九三：臀无肤，其行次且[6]，厉，无大咎。
九四：包无鱼，起凶。
九五：以杞包瓜[7]，含章，有陨自天[8]。
上九：姤其角[9]，吝；无咎。

Translation:

Meeting: (This) woman is so strong (as to be harmful to a man). Do not take her as a wife.

Six at the bottom line: Draw the bronze brake (to stop the carriage).

95

Good omen. Misfortune comes if one takes a trip. A pig is being tied, struggling with all its might.

Nine at the second line: There is fish in the kitchen. No disaster. But it is not appropriate to serve it to guests.

Nine at the third line: One acts with difficulties for one's haunches have been flayed. There will be danger but no serious calamity.

Nine at the fourth line: Trouble arises from the fact that there is no fish in the kitchen.

Nine at the fifth line: put a melon into a container made of willow branches. Something, with beauty hidden inside, falls from the heaven.

Nine at the top line: One is hurt when running into an animal horn. Some regret occurs but no disaster.

Notes:

1. 姤(gou): it is also written as 遘(gou) and in the *I Ching on Silk* is 狗(gou), signifying meeting. This hexagram is composed of five yang lines and one yin line, indicating that one woman meets five men.

2. 女壮, 勿用取女(nu zhuang, wu yong qu nu): do not marry this woman for she is so strong as to be harmful to a man. 壮(zhuang): strong or damage. 取(qu): marry.

3. 系于金柅(ji yu jin ni): draw the bronze brake of the carriage wheel to control its advance or stop it. 系(ji) is substituted by 击(ji) in the *I Ching on Silk*, meaning draw or drag. 柅(ni) is also written as 尼, and in the *I Ching on Silk* as 梯(ti). A variety of interpretations are available. They are gloom, brake of a cart, block, etc.. According to the interpretation of 象(Xiang), one of the ten *Appendixes to the I Ching*, we understand it as a brake.

4. 羸豕孚蹢躅(lei shi fu zhi zhu): tying a pig. 羸豕(lei shi): tie a pig with rope. 蹢躅(zhi zhu) is written as 适属(shi shu) in the *I Ching on Silk*, describing a pig's struggle when being tied.

5. 包有鱼，无咎，不利宾(bao you yu, wu jiu, bu li bin)：there is fish in the kitchen. No fault. But it is disadvantageous to entertain guests. 包(bao) is 庖, kitchen.

6. 臀无肤，其行次且(tun wu fu, qi xing ci qie)：one moves with difficulty for one's haunches have been flayed (see Hexagram Guai, Nine at the fourth line).

7. 以杞包瓜(yi qi bao gua)：put melon in a container made of willow branches. 杞(qi)：willow.

8. 含章，有陨自天(han zhang, you yun zi tian)：beauty hidden (in the melon), something falls from heaven. 章(zhang)：beauty; it is also interpreted as bright. 陨(yun)：fall. We adopt this interpretation from earlier scholars. But it seems that this line of the Hexagram tells this story: An object in a willow container is seen, with lights, falling to the ground. This is probably a record of an unidentified flying object.

9. 姤其角(gou qi jiao)：run into an animal horn and be hurt by it.

Hexagram 45
萃(Cui) Assembling

The Chinese text:

萃[1]：亨，王假有庙[2]，利见大人，亨，利贞。用大牲吉[3]。利有攸往。
初六：有孚不终，乃乱乃萃[4]。若号，一握为笑[5]。勿恤，往无咎。
六二：引吉，无咎[6]。孚乃利用禴[7]。
六三：萃如嗟如[8]。无攸利。往无咎，小吝。
九四：大吉，无咎。
九五：萃有位，无咎[9]。匪孚，元永贞，悔亡[10]。

97

上六：赍咨涕[11]，无咎。

Translation：

Assembling：Great success. The king reaches a temple and makes an offering. It is auspicious to meet a great man and remain faithful when one has a success. Offer great cattle and sheep as sacrifices. Advantageous to take a trip.

Six at the bottom line：One possesses sincerity but cannot maintain it to the last. Thus disorder and illness arise. Meeting with a good number when asking an oracle, one turns crying into laughter. No need to worry, just go there. No harm.

Six at the second line：No error to meet with good fortune. Be faithful and conduct the summer sacrifice for one's blessing.

Six at the third line：gathering together and sighing is unfavourable. No disaster but slight trouble follows if one travels.

Nine at the fourth line：Super fortune and no fault.

Nine at the fifth line：Gathering together with every one keeping correct position leads to no disaster. The regrets will disappear if an unfaithful person changes and begins to follow the principle of righteousness.

Six at the top line：One is so sorrowful for the missing money that one weeps abundantly. No disaster.

Notes：

1. 萃(cui)：assembling, gathering or illness. It is written as 卒(zu) in the *I Ching on Silk*.

2. 王假有庙(wang jia you miao)：the king arrives in the temple and makes an offering. 假(jia)：arrive in, reach.

3. 用大牲吉(yong da sheng ji)：auspicious to offer great sacrifice. 大牲(da sheng) denotes cattle or sheep as sacrifice.

4. 有孚不终，乃乱乃萃(you fu bu zhong, nai luan nai cui): if sincerity cannot be maintained to the end, confusion and disease will happen. 萃 (cui) means disease, illness here.

5. 若号，一握为笑(ruo hao, yi wo wei xiao): one cries at first and then laughs because one is given a fortunate number, *Yi Wo*, when consulting an oracle. 一握(yi wo) was a term for divination in ancient China, indicating a good number. This line says that one is in an unfortunate situation when one comes for divination. One turns crying into laughter when given the good number. 握(wo) is changed into 屋 (wu) in the *I Ching on Silk*.

6. 引吉，无咎(yin ji, wu jiu): meet with a lucky thing. No fault. 引 (yin): meet with, encounter.

7. 孚乃利用禴(fu nai li yong yue): be sincere and then make use of the Summer offering for one's bliss. 禴(yue) is written as 濯, identical to 躍. They all denote the spring and summer offerings in later Shang Dynasty.

8. 萃如嗟如(cui ru jie ru): gather and sigh. 嗟(jie): sigh.

9. 萃有位，无咎(cui you wei, wu jiu): gather together and everyone has his appropriate status. No disaster.

10. 匪孚，元永贞，悔亡(fei fu, yuan yong zhen, hui wang): regret may vanish if an unfaithful person changes and starts to observe the principle of righteousness.

11. 赍咨涕洟(zi zi ti yi): one is so sorrowful that tears are shed and nasal mucus flow when one's money is missing. 赍咨 (zi zi): lose money or property. 涕洟(ti yi): tear and nasal nucuses.

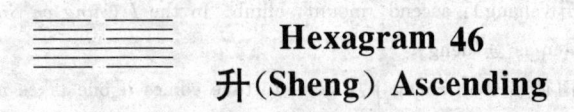

Hexagram 46
升(Sheng) Ascending

The Chinese text:

升[1]：元亨，用见大人，勿恤。南征吉[2]。
初六：允升，大吉[3]。
九二：孚乃利用禴，无咎。
九三：升虚邑[4]。
六四：王用亨于岐山[5]，吉，无咎。
六五：贞吉，升阶[6]。
上六：冥升，利于不息之贞[7]。

Translation:

Ascending: One starts with great success. It is advantageous to meet a great man. Get rid of your anxiety. Good fortune arises if one takes military action southward.

Six at the bottom line: Promotion is indeed a great good fortune.

Nine at the second line: One is faithful and therefore it is alright to make the Summer offering to seek abiding well-being. No harm.

Nine at the third line: Climb to the top of a high hill.

Six at the fourth line: The king made a sacrifice on Mount Qi. Good fortune and no disaster.

Six at the fifth line: It is auspicious to remain steadfastly faithful. One will be promoted step by step.

Six at the top line: Climbing in darkness, one ought to follow the right way with no alteration.

Notes:

1. 升 (sheng): ascend, mount, climb. In the *I Ching on Silk* it is written as 登 (deng).

2. 南征吉 (nan zheng ji): good fortune comes if one takes military action southwards.

3. 允升，大吉 (yun sheng, da ji): being promoted to a higher position is great good fortune. 允 (yun): promotion, advance.

100

4. 升虛邑 (sheng xu yi): go up to the city on the high hill. 升 (sheng): go up, mount. 虛 (xu): hill.

5. 王用亨于岐山 (wang yong heng yu qi shan): the king made an offering on Mount Qi. 亨 (heng): to offer sacrifice. 岐山 (qi shan): name of a mountain in the northeast of Qishan County, Shanxi Province.

6. 貞吉，升階 (zhen ji, sheng jie): fortunate if one is faithful. One will be promoted step by step.

7. 冥升，利于不息之貞 (ming sheng, li yu bu xi zhi zhen): ascending in darkness, one should walk along the right way without change. 冥 (ming): dakness. 貞 (zhen): be steadily faithful.

Hexagram 47
困 (Kun) Adversity

The Chinese text:

困¹：亨，貞，大人吉，无咎。有言不信²。
初六：臀困于株木³，入于幽谷，三歲不覿⁴。
九二：困于酒食，朱紱方來⁵，利用亨祀。征凶。无咎。
六三：困于石，據于蒺藜⁶。入于其宮，不見其妻⁷，凶。
九四：來徐徐，困于金車⁸，吝，有終。
九五：劓刖，困于赤紱⁹。乃徐有說¹⁰，利用祭祀。
上六：困于葛藟，于臲卼¹¹，曰動悔¹²，有悔，征吉。

Translation:

Adversity: Great success. A favourable divination for a great man. No calamity. When one is in adversity, others do not believe what one

101

says.

Six at the bottom line: One is entangled by tree branches and trapped in a gloomy valley without seeing any person for three years.

Nine at the second line: When drunk, a red garment is given. One wears it for the ceremony of offering sacrifice. It shows danger but no serious trouble will occur when one takes military action.

Six at the third line: The confused rocks are in one's way and thistles and briars are found everywhere. Entering one's mansion, one fails to find one's wife. Misfortune.

Nine at the fourth line: One comes slowly because some troubles was with one's golden carriage on the way. The end will be good in spite of the troubles earlier.

Nine at the fifth line: One is punished by having one's nose cut off and leg broken because of wearing the red clothes. Thus one takes them off slowly. It is advantageous to offer sacrifice.

Six at the top line: Entangled by plant vines and grasses, one is anxious. Thinking of action will lead to regret. No disaster but some slight regrets happen if one takes military action.

Notes:

1. 困(kun): adversity, hardship, trouble.

2. 有言不信(you yan bu xin): (in adversity) one speaks but no one believes. 信(xin): believe, trust.

3. 臀困于株木(tun kun yu zhu mu): one's haunches are entangled by the tree branches. 株(zhu): tree branch, dried tree, or tree root; in this case, it refers to a tree branch.

4. 三岁不觌(san sui bu di): cannot see others for three years. 岁(sui): year. 觌(di): see.

5. 困于酒食,朱绂方来(kun yu jiu shi, zhu fu fang lai): one was given the red ceremonial garment when drunk. 困于酒食(kun yu jiu shi): drunk. 朱绂(zhu fu): garment for making offerings in the temple

or clothes specially for a king. Here it means the former.

6. 困于石，据于蒺藜(kun yu shi, ju yu ji li)：rocks are in one's way and thistles and briars are everywhere. 困于石(kun yu shi)：rocks in the way or one is blocked by the rocks. 据(ju)：occupied, entangled.

7. 入于其宫，不见其妻(ru yu qi gong, bu jian qi qi)：when entering one's mansion, one fails to find one's wife. 宫（gong）：mansion, palace, dwelling place in general.

8. 来徐徐，困于金车(lai xu xu, kun yu jin che)：be delayed by troubles with one's golden carriage. 徐徐（xu xu）：calm and slow movement. 困于金车(kun yu jin che)：a problem with one's golden cart.

9. 劓刖，困于赤绂(yi yue, kun yu chi fu)：nose cutting and leg breaking were brought about by one's wearing a red garment. 劓(yi)：nose cutting; a punishment in ancient China. 刖(yue)：breaking one's leg, a punishment in ancient China.

10. 乃徐有说（nai xu you tuo）：therefore one took off the (red garment) slowly.

11. 困于葛藟，于臲卼(kun yu ge lei, yu nie wu)：entangled by some plant vines and grasses, one is anxious. 葛藟（ge lei）：vines and grass. 臲卼(nie wu)：describing one's anxiety.

12. 曰动悔(yue dong hui)：to plan an action will results in regret. 曰(yue)：think, plan.

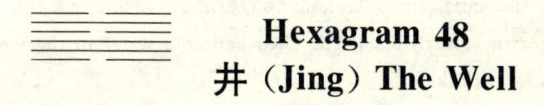

Hexagram 48
井（Jing）The Well

The Chinese text：

井¹：改邑不改井²，无丧无得。往来井井³，汔至，亦未繘井⁴，羸其瓶⁵，

103

凶。

初六：井泥不食，旧井无禽[6]。

九二：井谷射鲋，瓮敝漏[7]。

九三：井渫不食[8]，为我心恻，可用汲[9]，王明，并受其福[10]。

六四：井甃[11]，无咎。

九五：井冽，寒泉食[12]。

上六：井收勿幕[13]，有孚元吉[14]。

Translation：

The Well：The well cannot be moved away when the households of the village have moved. Thus (the well) does not lose，nor gains. The people come to and fro to take water from the well. The well has become dry but it has not been dug out by anyone. As a result，the water bucket is damaged. Misfortune.

Six at the bottom line：There is nothing but mud in the well. The muddy water cannot be drunk. Even the birds cease flight around the well.

Nine at the second line：While shooting at the fish in the well bottom, one damaged one's bucket.

Nine at the third line：I am sad that the people have not taken water from the well which has been restored. The well can be used now because of the wise king with whom everyone shares his favours and grace.

Six at the fourth line：No fault to repair the well.

Nine at the fourth line：The clear and cold water in the well can be taken and drunk.

Six at the top line：No need to cover the well when the water has been taken out. Good fortune follows when the well resumes.

Notes：

1. 井 (jing)：a well；also a social unit like a small village in ancient

China consisting of eight households.

2. 改邑不改井(gai yi bu gai jing): the small village may be moved but the well cannot. 改(gai): change, move.

3. 往来井井(wang lai jing jing): shuttling to and fro to fetch water from the well.

4. 汔至, 亦未繘井(qi zhi, yi wei ju jing): the well has become dry, but no one digs it out. 汔(qi): water has evaporated, dry. 繘(ju): to string, or a rope used to pull a water bucket from the well.

5. 羸其瓶(lei qi ping): the water bucket is damaged. 羸(lei): damage; it is written as 累(lei) in the *I Ching on Silk*. 瓶(ping): bucket used to take water.

6. 旧井无禽(jiu jing wu qin): there are no birds around the well. Two different interpretations are available as follows: first, in ancient times the people used to plant trees beside the well which attract birds. Thus the birds did not come when the well was damaged and the trees withered. Second, birds are used to building nests in the well. When the well becomes old, it is not suitable to build nests, therefore birds do not come.

7. 井谷射鲋, 瓮敝漏(jing gu she fu, weng bi lou): while shooting at the fish at the well bottom, one's water pot is damaged. 谷(gu): bottom. 鲋(fu): little fish. 瓮(weng): water pot, bucket. This sentence is written as 井渎射付唯敝句(jing du she fu wei bi ju) in the *I ching on Silk*, the meaning is slightly different.

8. 井渫不食(jing xie bu shi): no one takes water to drink from the well though it has been cleaned up. 渫(xie): to repair, to make the dirty water clean.

9. 为我心恻, 可用汲(wei wo xin ce, ke yong ji): I am sad that no one takes water to drink from this well. 恻(ce): sad, compassionate.

10. 王明, 并受其福(wang ming, bing shou qi fu): all the people under the heavens share the favours and grace from the wise king. 明(ming): wise and able.

11. 井甃(jing zhou): to repair the well. It is sustituted by 椒 in the *I Ching on Silk*. Another interpretation is to build the wall of a well.

12. 井洌，寒泉食(jing lie, han quan shi): the clear and cold water in the well can be drunk. 洌(lie): clear and cold. 寒泉(han quan): cold water in the well, the source of which was considered to be the springs in the underground.

13. 井收勿幕(jing shou wu mu): do not need to cover the well when one has taken water out of it. 收 (shou): take water with a winch. 幕 (mu): cover, lid.

14. 有孚元吉(you fu yuan ji): good fortune arises when the well resumes after repair. 孚(fu): resume, restore; it is written as 復 in the *I Ching on Silk*.

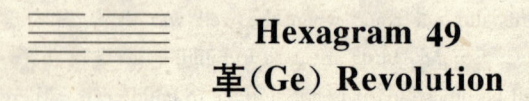

Hexagram 49
革(Ge) Revolution

The Chinese text:

革¹：巳日乃孚²。元亨利贞，悔亡。

初九：巩用黄牛之革³。

六二：巳日乃革之⁴，征吉，无咎。

九三：征凶，贞厉。革言三就⁵，有孚。

九四：悔亡。有孚，改命吉⁶。

九五：大人虎变。未占有孚⁷。

上六：君子豹变，小人革面⁸，征凶。居贞吉。

Translation:

Revolution: Keep faith in revolution on the day of the sixth of the

Heavenly Stems. It is advantageous to stick to the principle of faithfulness when starting with success. Regrets vanish.

Nine at the bottom line: Tie it fast with leather made from a yellow ox.

Six at the second line: Do not put the revolutionary strategy into practice until the day of the sixth of the Heavenly Stems. It is auspicious to take military action. No disaster.

Nine at the third line: It is dangerous to lead an army to fight. The divination shows danger, thus it is necessary to discuss and calculate repeatedly before taking revolutionary action. Do have firm faith.

Nine at the fourth line: Regrets disappear. Remain faithful. Auspicious to change the existing dynasty.

Nine at the fifth line: During the revolution the great man is as brave and powerful as a tiger. He shows faithfulness before consulting an oracle.

Six at the top line: During the revolution the superior man moves as rapidly as a leopard; even ordinary persons change their normal behaviour. It is misfortune to take military action. Do not move and good fortune will arise.

Notes:

1. 革(ge): revolution, reform or overthrow the existing dynasty.
2. 巳日乃孚(si ri nai fu): it is a good time to start revolution on the sixth of the ten Heavenly Stems when the zenith period has passed. 巳(si) is synonymous with 己(ji), the day of the sixth of the Heavenly Stems.
3. 巩用黄牛之革(gong yong huang niu zhi ge): to tie with leather made from a yellow ox. 巩(gong): to strengthen, to tie. 革(ge): leather.
4. 巳日乃革之(si ri nai ge zhi): to revolt on the day of the sixth of the Heavenly Stems.

5. 革言三就(ge yan san jiu): the great revolution must be taken so seriously and prudently that it should not be decided before repeated discussions and calculations. 就(jiu): calculation.

6. 有孚，改命吉(you fu, gai ming ji): be sincere. Auspicious to change the dynasty.

7. 大人虎变，未占有孚(da ren hu bian, wei zhan you fu): a great man is as brave and powerful as a tiger during the revolution. He is known to be faithful before consulting his fortune. 虎变(hu bian): change greatly like a tiger ridding itself of its seasonal coat.

8. 君子豹变，小人革面(jun zi bao bian, xiao ren ge mian): during the revolution, a superior man moves as rapidly as a leopard; even the common people are forced to change their behavours. 豹变(bao bian): change like a leopard. From this hexagram we learn that the superior man is lower than the great man just as the leopard is lower than the tiger.

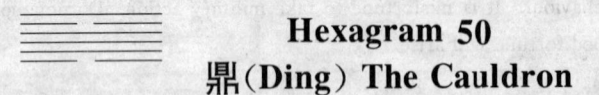

Hexagram 50
鼎(Ding) The Cauldron

The Chinese text:

鼎[1]：元吉，亨。

初六：鼎颠趾，利出否[2]，得妾以其子[3]，无咎。

九二：鼎有实，我仇有疾，不我能即[4]，吉。

九三：鼎耳革，其行塞[5]，雉膏不食，方雨亏悔[6]，终吉。

九四：鼎折足，覆公餗，其形渥[7]，凶。

六五：鼎黄耳，金铉[8]，利贞。

上九：鼎玉铉，大吉[9]，无不利。

108

Translation:

Cauldron: Good fortune at the beginning. Sublime success.

Six at the bottom line: The cauldron is turned upside down and one should drive out one's wife. It is faultless to take a concubine for the sake of bearing children.

Nine at the second line: The cauldron is filled with food. My wife is sick and she is not able to approach me. Good omen.

Nine at the third line: It is difficult to move the cauldron because its ears are detached. Thus the good food in it cannot be eaten. It rained a moment ago and now the cloud has dispersed. Good fortune comes in the end.

Nine at the fourth line: As the legs of the cauldron are broken, the prince's delicious food is overturned and spread everywhere. Misfortune.

Six at the fifth line: The cauldron has brass ears and handles. It is advantageous to keep the principle of steadfast faithfulness.

Nine at the top line: The cauldron possesses jade handles. Great fortune and nothing is disadvantageous.

Notes:

1. 鼎 (ding): a cauldron. It was a kind of cooking pot having three short legs and two ears made of brass. In the Shang and Zhou Dynasties it was so popular that it even became a symbol of royal power. This hexagram looks like a cauldron: the bottom line can be regarded as its legs; the fifth line signifies its ears; and the top line is like a handle. In this hexagram, the lower trigram symbolizes wood and the top one represents fire. This feature also shows that the cauldron is a cooking pot with fire underneath.

2. 鼎颠趾，利出否 (ding dian zhi, li chu fou): the cauldron is turned

upside down. It implies that one should drive one's wife out of the home. 出妇 (chu fu): drive out or divorce one's wife. This phrase is followed by a couplet " take a concubine " in the next phrase. In the *I Ching on Silk*, hexagram 否 (Pi) is replaced by 妇 (fu), which also proves that the two characters were identical with each other in classical Chinese and that 出否 (chu fou) means to drive out one's wife.

3. 得妾以其子 (de qie yi qi zi): take a concubine for the sake of bearing children.

4. 鼎有实，我仇有疾，不我能即 (ding you shi, wo chou you ji, bu wo neng ji): the cauldron is filled with food. My wife is ill so that she may not approach me. 仇 (chou): wife, match. 即 (ji): approach.

5. 鼎耳革，其行塞 (ding er ge, qi xing sai): it is hard to move the cauldron because the ears of the cauldron are missing. 革 (ge): detach, be missing. 塞 (sai): obstructed. Here it means difficulty in movement.

6. 雉膏不食，方雨亏悔 (zhi gao bu shi, fang yu kui hui): the delicious meat cannot be eaten. It rained just now and the cloud is gone. 雉膏 (zhi gao): food made of pheasant meat. 方 (fang): just now, a moment ago. 亏 (kui): decrease, reduce. 悔 (hui): cloud.

7. 鼎折足，覆公餗，其形渥 (ding zhe zu, fu gong su, qi xing wo): the prince's food is overturned and spread everywhere as the feet of the cauldron are broken. 餗 (su): a sort of delicious food made of valuable ingredients. 形渥 (xing wo): messy appearance of the overturned food.

8. 鼎黄耳，金铉 (ding huang er, jin xuan): the cauldron has brass ears and bronze handles. 黄耳 (huang er): ear made of brass. 金铉 (jin xuan): handle made of bronze.

9. 鼎玉铉，大吉 (ding yu xuan, da ji): the cauldron possesses jade handles. Great fortune. 玉铉 (yu xuan): handle made of jade.

Hexagram 51
震（Zhen）Thunder

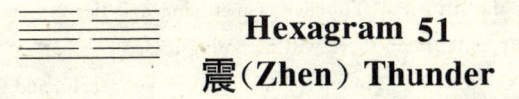

The Chinese text：

震¹：亨，震来虩虩，笑言哑哑²，震惊百里，不丧匕鬯³。
初九：震来虩虩，后笑言哑哑，吉。
六二：震来厉，亿丧贝⁴。跻于九陵，勿逐，七日得⁵。
六三：震苏苏，震行无眚⁶。
九四：震遂泥⁷。
六五：震往来厉，意无丧，有事。
上六：震索索，视矍矍⁸，征凶。震不于其躬，于其邻⁹，无咎。婚媾有言¹⁰。

Translation：

Thunder：Great success. Thunder rumbles and people tremble. However the one who offers the sacrifice still talks and laughs as usual. Lightning is striking and threatening for a hundred miles, but the maker of the sacrifice is so calm that the wine in the spoon in his hand is not spilt.
Nine at the bottom line：The people tremble when thunder sounds and then they resume natural talk and laughter. Auspicious.
Six at the second line：The threatening thunder rumbles fiercely. One is afraid to lose money. Climb to a high mountain and do not search for the lost money for it will return by itself in seven days.
Six at the third line：Thunder causes men to tremble fearfully. But no danger for the man walking in the rain when thunder rumbles and

111

lightning striks.

Nine at the fourth line: Lightning strikes falls to the mud.

Six at the fifth line: Thunder is menacing and fierce. Some accidents will happen althogh there will be no big loss.

Six at the top line: Thunder's noise makes men fearful and uneasy; the flashing light is so bright as not to be watched directly. It is unfavourable to take military action. Lightning does not strikes one's body but strikes one's neighbour. No disaster but some gossip arises about one's marriage.

Notes:

1. 震(zhen): thunder. Its extended meaning is trembling. In the *I Ching on Silk* it is written as 辰(chen).

2. 震来虩虩，笑言哑哑(zhen lai xi xi, xiao yan ya ya): the thunder and flashes occur and it is frightening. (But the leading worshiper) is talking and laughing as if nothing happened. 虩虩(xi xi): frightening or fearful; they are synonyms of 愬愬(su su). 哑哑(ya ya): the sound of laughter.

3. 震惊百里，不丧匕鬯(zhen jing bai li, bu sang bi chang): the thunder causes people to tremble for a hundred miles, but the leading worshiper is so calm that the sacrificial wine in his spoon is not spilt. 丧(sang): spilt, drop. 匕(bi): spoon with a wooden handle. When offering sacrifices, the offerer takes the cooked meat with it from the cauldron and puts the meat into a big container for the use of the great ceremony. 鬯(chang): a sort of sacrificial wine. 匕鬯(bi chang) is written as 钆觞 in the *I Ching on Silk*.

4. 震来厉，亿丧贝(zhen lai li, yi sang bei): the thunder is fierce and the lightning dangerous. (It is not a good omen,) it is afraid that one will lose money. 厉(li): danger. 亿(yi) is substituted in the *I Ching on Silk* by 意(yi), meaning in one's expectation or estimate. 贝(bei): money in ancient China.

5. 跻于九陵，勿逐，七日得(ji yu jiu ling, wu zhu, qi ri de): mount to the top of a high montain and do not look for the missing money. It will come back itself. 跻(ji): to mount, climb. 九陵(jiu ling): high mountain.

6. 震苏苏，震行无眚(zhen su su, zhen xing wu sheng): the thunder is terribly threatening. However, there will be no danger in walking when thunder is happening.

7. 震遂泥(zhen sui ni): lightning strikes the mud. 遂(sui): drop, fall or cease.

8. 震索索，视矍矍(zhen suo suo, shi jue jue): the thunder is rumbles and the flash is too bright to look at. 索索(suo suo): trembling and fearful. 矍矍(jue jue): cannot look at directly.

9. 震不于其躬，于其邻(zhen bu yu qi gong, yu qi lin): the lightning does not strike one's body but strikes one's neighbour. 躬(gong): body. 邻(lin): neighbour.

10. 婚媾有言(hun gou you yan): the marriage gives rise to some gossip. 言(yan): gossip, blame.

Hexagram 52
艮(Gen) Keeping Still

The Chinese text:

艮[1]：艮其背，不获其身[2]，行其庭，不见其人[3]。无咎。

初六：艮其趾[4]，无咎，利永贞。

六二：艮其腓[5]，不拯其随[6]，其心不快[7]。

九三：艮其限[8]、列其夤[9]，厉薰心[10]。

六四：艮其身，无咎。

六五：艮其辅，言有序¹¹，悔亡。
上九：敦艮¹²，吉。

Translation：

Keeping Still：The whole body cannot move if one's back is still. One walks in the courtyard without seeing anyone else. No disaster.

Six at the bottom line：One's toes stiffen. No trouble. It is advantageous to be steadfastly faithful.

Six at the second line：While the calves cannot move, one cannot raise one's legs and one is deeply unhappy.

Nine at the third line：One's waist stills and the flesh on one's back is torn off. One is anxious with a burning fear about the danger.

Six at the fourth line：No disaster if one's body cannot move.

Six at the fifth line：One speaks in order without moving one's cheeks. No regret will arise.

Nine at the top line：It is auspicious if one knows when to limit honesty.

Notes：

1. 艮 (gen)：stop, cease. In the *I Ching on Silk* it is replaced by 根 (gen).

2. 艮其背，不获其身 (gen qi bei, bu huo qi shen)：one's back stiffen. As a result, one's whole body cannot move either.

3. 行其庭，不见其人 (xing qi ting, bu jian qi ren)：walking in the courtyard, without seeing anyone in it. 庭 (ting)：courtyard.

4. 艮其趾 (gen qi zhi)：toes cannot move. 趾 (zhi)：toe; it is written as 止 (zhi) in the *I Ching on Silk*.

5. 艮其腓 (gen qi fei)：one's calves cannot move. 腓 (fei)：calf.

6. 不拯其随 (bu zheng qi sui)：one cannot lift one's legs. 拯 (zheng)：lift, raise.

7. 其心不快(qi xin bu kuai): unhappy from one's heart.
8. 艮其限(gen qi xian): one's waist stiffens. 限(xian): waist.
9. 列其夤(lie qi yin): the flesh near the spine is torn off. 列(lie): is identical to 裂 (lie), torn. It is written as 戾(li) in the *I Ching on Silk*. 夤(yin): the flesh on the back.
10. 厉薰心(li xun xin): one's heart is burning with anxiety about danger. 厉(li): danger and emergency. 薰(xun): burn.
11. 艮其辅, 言有序(gen qi fu, yan you xu): two cheeks are still, but one can say words in good order. 辅(fu): cheeks. 序(xu): in good order or sequence.
12. 敦艮(dun gen): honesty rests. 敦(dun): honesty.

Hexagram 53
渐 (Jian) Gradual Progress

The Chinese text:

渐[1]: 女归[2], 吉, 利贞。
初六: 鸿渐于干[3], 小子厉, 有言[4], 无咎。
六二: 鸿渐于磐, 饮食衎衎[5], 吉。
九三: 鸿渐于陆, 夫征不复[6], 妇孕不育, 凶。利御寇[7]。
六四: 鸿渐于木, 或得其桷[8], 无咎。
九五: 鸿渐于陵[9], 妇三岁不孕, 终莫之胜[10], 吉。
上九: 鸿渐于陆, 其羽可用为仪[11], 吉。

Translation:

Gradual Progress: It is auspicious for a maiden to marry and follow the principle of steadfast faithfulness.

115

Six at the bottom line: A wild swan moves to the river bank. It implies that a youngster will face a danger and be blamed. But there will be no big trouble for him.

Six at the second line: The wild swan approaches a rock and rests on it, enjoying drink and food. Good fortune.

Nine at the third line: The wild swan moves to a plateau and stays there. It indicates that the husband will never be back when he is sent forth to fight. His wife is pregnant without giving birth in time. Misfortune. It is advantageous to defend against robbers.

Six at the fourth line: Swans move to a wood and rest there. Some of them perch on a log. No harm.

Nine at the fifth line: Swans fly to a hill. The wife cannot conceive for three years. One cannot win in the end. It is faultless.

Nine at the top line: A swan rests on a plateau. Its feather can be used as an ornament. Good fortune.

Notes:

1. 渐 (jian): gradual progress. This hexagram is about a girl's marriage.

2. 女归 (nu gui): a maiden marries. 归 (gui): a girl's marriage.

3. 鸿渐于干 (hong jian yu gan): a wild swan moves gradually to the bank of a river. 鸿 (hong): a wild swan or a wild goose. 干 (gan): river bank. A different interpretation of 干 (gan) is a stream flowing down from a mountain.

4. 小子厉，有言 (xiao zi li, you yan): a youngster is in danger. His behavour gives rise to some scandals but no disaster. 厉 (li): danger, trouble. 言 (yan): gossip, scandal.

5. 鸿渐于磐，饮食衎衎 (hong jian yu pan, yin shi kan kan): the swan approaches and rests near a rock, eating and drinking, pleased. 磐 (pan): big rock; it is also written as 般 (ban) or 坂 (ban) in classical Chinese. 衎衎 (kan kan): happy, pleased.

6. 鸿渐于陆，夫征不复(hong jian yu lu, fu zheng bu fu)：a wild swan moves to a high land and rests on it. The husband (who encounters this hexagram)will never return if he goes out to battle. 陆(lu)：high land, plateau.

7. 妇孕不育，凶，利御寇 (fu yun bu yu, xiong, li yu kou)：the pregnant wife cannot give birth. Misfortune. But it is advantageous to resist robbers. 御(yu)：resist, defend against.

8. 鸿渐于木，或得其桷(hong jian yu mu, huo de qi jue)：some swans rest on a tree； and some perch on a log. 或（huo）：someone, sometime. 桷(jue)：a log above the house beam to support tiles. In the State of Qin, it was called 椽(chuan) and 桷(jue) was its name in the States of Qi and Lu.

9. 鸿渐于陵(hong jian yu ling)：the wild swans approach a hill and rest on it. 陵(ling)：hill, mountain.

10. 终莫之胜(zhong mo zhi sheng)：not win in the end. 莫(mo)：no, cannot.

11. 其羽可用为仪(qi yu ke yong wei yi)：its feather can be used in decoration. 仪(yi)：decoration, ornament.

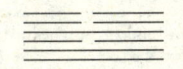

Hexagram 54
归妹(Gui Mei) Marrying Maiden

The Chinese text：

归妹[1]：征凶，无攸利。
初九：归妹以娣，跛能履[2]，征吉。
九二：眇能视，利幽人之贞[3]。
六三：归妹以须，反归以娣[4]。

117

九四：归妹愆期，迟归有时[5]。

六五：帝乙归妹，其君之袂不如其娣之袂良[6]。月几望[7]，吉。

上六：女承筐无实[8]，士刲羊无血[9]。无攸利。

Translation：

Marrying Maiden：Advance brings misfortune. Nothing is advantageous.

Nine at the bottom line：The maiden marries and her sister accompanies her as a concubine. A person with a lame leg can walk. It is auspicious to take military action.

Nine at the second line：A person with a blind eye can see. This line is favourable to a prisoner.

Six at the third line：The maiden marries and her elder sister accompanies her as a concubine. But when they return to their own home the maiden (younger sister) becomes a concubine.

Nine at the fourth line：The maiden's marriage is postponed for the sake of waiting.

Six at the fifth line：King Yi arranged his daughter's marriage. The bride's clothes are not so beautiful as the accompanying sister's. The sixteenth is chosen as the auspicious day for marriage.

Six at the top line：The marriageable lady holds a basket without dowry. A young man stabs a sheep but no blood is shed. Nothing is favourable.

Notes：

1. 归妹(gui mei)：maiden's marriage to a man. 归(gui)：marriage of a maiden. 妹(mei)：maiden, girl.

2. 归妹以娣，跛能履(gui mei yi di, po neng lu)：a sister of the marrying maiden follows her to marry the same man. A person with a lame leg can walk. 娣(di)：the accompanying sister of the marrying

girl. Polygamy was adopted in ancient China. According to this system a sister of the marriageable maiden may accompany her to marry the same man as his concubine; the marriage of the concubine-sister is called 娣(di). This custom was still popular in the Spring and Autumn period.

3. 眇能视，利幽人之贞(miao neng shi, li you ren zhi zhen): a person with a blind eye can see. This hexagram is favourable to a prisoner.

4. 归妹以须，反归以娣(gui mei yi xu, fan gui yi di): the elder sister as a concubine follows the younger sister to marry a husband. But when they return to their parents' home, the elder sister becomes wife and the younger a companion as a concubine. 须(xu) is also written as 嬃, meaning concubine. 反(fan): return to the parents' home from the husband's.

5. 归妹愆期，迟归有时(gui mei yan qi, chi gui you shi): the maiden's marriage is delayed for the sake of waiting. 愆(yan) is identical to 衍 (yan) in the *I Ching on Silk*, meaning delay, postpone. 迟(chi): later. 时(shi) is synonymous to 伺(si), wait.

6. 其君之袂不如其娣之袂良(qi jun zhi mei bu ru qi di zhi mei liang): the clothes of the wife are not so beautiful as those of her concubine-sister. 袂(mei): jacket sleeve; here it denotes clothes.

7. 月几望(yue ji wang): the sixteenth day of every lunar month.

8. 女承筐无实(nu cheng kuang wu shi): the marrying maiden's basket is short of dowry. 女(nu) the marriageable girl. 筐(kuang): dowry-basket of the bride.

9. 士刲羊无血(shi kui yang wu xie): in the wedding a young man stabs the lamb without drawing blood. 士(shi): young man. 刲(kui): stab, cut.

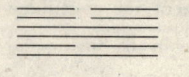

Hexagram 55
丰(Feng)：Abundance

The Chinese text：

丰¹：亨，王假之²，勿忧，宜日中³。
初九：遇其配主⁴，虽旬无咎，往有尚⁵。
六二：丰其蔀，日中见斗⁶。往得疑疾，有孚发若⁷。吉。
九三：丰其沛，日中见沫⁸，折其右肱⁹，无咎。
九四：丰其蔀，日中见斗，遇其夷主¹⁰，吉。
六五：来章，有庆誉¹¹，吉。
上六：丰其屋，蔀其家¹²，阙其户，阒其无人¹³，三岁不觌¹⁴，凶。

Translation：

Abundance：The King is present at the ceremony of sacrifice when it takes place. Do not fear. It is advantageous to hold the ceremony at noon.

Nine at the bottom line：One meets with the chief of the Pei nation. No disaster arises in the next ten days. One will be granted a reward when going forward.

Six at the second line：The daylight is completely covered and stars are visible at midday. One will suffer illness if one goes there. But the disease will be cured if one remains sincere and faithful. Good fortune.

Nine at the third line：It becomes darker and darker and the darkness occurs at noon. One breaks one's right arm in the darkness. But no serious calamity will happen.

Nine at the fourth line：The daylight is completely covered and stars appear at noon. It is auspicious to encounter the chief of the Xirong nation.

Nine at the fifth line: The sunlight is visible again. People celebrate it with great joy. Good fortune.

Six at the top line: There is a large house which is covered with shadow. Watching its door and window, one finds nobody except the quiet and empty rooms. Nothing has been found in it in the past three years. Misfortune.

Notes:

1. 丰(feng): abundance and splendor.
2. 亨, 王假之(heng, wang jia zhi): the king lends his presence at the ceremony of making sacrifice. 亨(heng): offering sacrifice. 假(jia): be present, arrive. It is written as 叚 in the *I Ching on Silk*.
3. 勿忧, 宜日中(wu you, yi ri zhong): do not worry. It is fitting to take place at noon. 日中(ri zhong): at noon.
4. 遇其配主(yu qi pei zhu): encounter the chief of Pei nation. 配主(pei zhu) has been given various interpretations like consort or matcher, which are not convincing. According to the text of the *I Ching on Silk*, in which 配(pei) is substituted by 肥(fei), and considering the related phrase 夷主(yi zhu) in the fourth line of this hexagram, we hold that 配(pei) is 肥(fei) which was a branch of White Di, an ethnic minority in the Spring and Autumn period and now spread throughout Shanxi and Hebei Provinces.
5. 虽旬无咎, 往有尚(sui xun wu jiu, wang you shang): no disaster comes in next ten days. One might be bestowed a reward if going there. 虽(sui) is rewritten in the *I Ching on Silk* as 唯(wei), meaning only. 旬(xun): every ten days counting from the first day of a month. Thus 虽旬(sui xun) can be correctly interpreted as only ten days. 尚(shang): reward.
6. 丰其蔀, 日中见斗(feng qi pou, ri zhong jian dou): the sunlight is completely covered and the stars are visible at midday. 丰(feng):

vastly, greaty. 蔀(pou): somthing covering sunlight. 斗(dou): stars in the sky.

7. 往得疑疾,有孚发若(wang de yi ji, you fu fa ruo):going forward, one suffers disease. But the illness will vanish if one is sincere and faithful. 发(fa): vanish, remove.

8. 丰其沛,日中见沫(feng qi pei, ri zhong jian mo): the sky becomes deeply dark and lights are not seen at midday. 沛(pei) is written as 旆 in the *I Ching on Silk*, meaning darkness without any light. 沫(mo): obscure and dark. This line must be the record of a solar eclipse.

9. 折其右肱(zhe qi you gong): one's right arm is broken.

10. 遇其夷主(yu qi yi zhu): meet with the chief of Xirong nation. 夷(yi): ethnic minority.

11. 来章,有庆誉(lai zhang, you qing yu): lights appear again and the people celebrate it with great joy. 章(zhang): light, bright.

12. 丰其屋,蔀其家(feng qi wu, pou qi jia): the house is large but one's home is covered with shadow.

13. 闚其户,闃其无人(kui qi hu, qu qi wu ren):inspecting the door and window, one finds nobody in the quiet and empty house. 闚(kui): look at, inspect. 闃(qu): quiet and empty.

14. 三岁不觌(san sui bu di): nothing has been seen in the past three years. 觌(di): see.

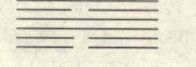

Hexagram 56
旅(Lu) The Traveller

The Chinese text:

旅[1]:小亨,旅,贞吉。

初六：旅琐琐², 斯其所取灾³。
六二：旅即次, 怀其资⁴, 得童仆贞⁵。
九三：旅焚其次⁶, 丧其童仆贞, 厉。
九四：旅于处, 得其资斧⁷, 我心不快。
六五：射雉, 一矢亡⁸, 终以誉命⁹。
上九：鸟焚其巢, 旅人先笑后号咷¹⁰, 丧牛于易¹¹, 凶。

Translation:

The Traveller: Success in small affairs. It will be auspicious if one is righteous during one's travels.

Six at the bottom line: One's petty and mean behavour during travel results in disaster.

Six at the second line: The traveller reaches and lives in an inn with money in his robe. He is treated well by a loyal servant.

Nine at the third line: The traveller burns the inn and the servant is missing. He is facing serious danger.

Nine at the fourth line: When frustrated in travel one obtains a sacred ax, which makes me jealous.

Six at the fifth line: One loses an arrow because one shoots at a pheasant and misses the target. But one gains fame and a noble title in the end.

Nine at the top line: The bird nest has been burned and an ox has been lost in the grain ground. The traveller laughs first and then cries and shouts.

Notes:

1. 旅(lu): traveller or an army; originally meant two persons.
2. 旅琐琐(lu suo suo): humble and mean while travelling.
3. 斯其所取灾(si qi suo qu zai): this brings disaster. 斯(si): this.
4. 旅即次, 怀其资(lu ji ci, huai qi zi): live in an inn with money in

one's robe. 即(ji): arrive at and live. 次(ci): hotel, inn. 怀(huai):in one's garment. 资(zi): money.

5. 得童仆贞(de tong pu zhen): gain a loyal servant. 童仆(tong pu): servant or slave.

6. 旅焚其次(lu fen qi ci): the traveller burns the inn. 焚(fen):burn.

7. 旅于处, 得其资斧(lu yu chu, de qi zi fu): frustrated while travelling, one is granted a sacred ax. 处(chu): cease, stop. 资斧(zi fu) was interpreted in the Han Dynasty as 齐斧(qi fu); in classical Chinese, 齐(qi) and 斋(zhai) could be used as synonyms. When one led an army to fight, one entered a temple and accepted a holy ax as a symbol of power. When military action ended the commander returned it to the monarch in the temple.

8. 射雉, 一矢亡(she zhi, yi shi wang): shooting at a pheasant, one loses an arrow. 雉(zhi): pheasant. 亡(wang): lose, miss.

9. 终以誉命(zhong yi yu ming): gain renown and a noble title ultimately. 命(ming): title, rank.

10. 旅人先笑后号咷(lu ren xian xiao hou hao tao): the traveller laughs first and then shouts and weeps. 号咷(hao tao): cry, weep.

11. 丧牛于易(sang niu yu yi): one's ox is missing in the grain ground.

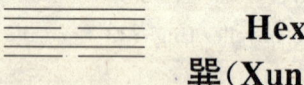

Hexagram 57
巽(Xun) Calculation

The Chinese text:

巽[1]: 小亨, 利有攸往, 利见大人。
初六: 进退, 利武人之贞[2]。

九二：巽在床下，用史巫纷若³，吉，无咎。
九三：频巽⁴，吝。
六四：悔亡，田获三品⁵。
九五：贞吉，悔亡，无不利，无初有终⁶。先庚三日，后庚三日⁷，吉。
上九：巽在床下，丧其资斧⁸，贞凶。

Translation:

Calculation: Succeess in small matters. It is advantageous to take a trip and meet a great man.

Six at the bottom line: A military man hesitates to advance or retreat. He is right to observe the principle of faithfulness.

Nine at the second line: The fortune-teller does divination under a bed. The officials of sacrifice and witches also help him to drive away the demons. End well and disaster is avoided.

Nine at the third line: Trouble arises if one frequently consults oracles.

Six at the fourth line: Regret disappears. Three kinds of game have been obtained in hunting.

Nine at the fifth line: Auspicious if one remains steadily faithful. Regrets vanish and nothing is disadvantageous. Unsuccessful at first (on the date of the first of the Heavenly Stems) but end well at last (on the day of the tenth of the Heavenly Stems). The auspicious days are the fourth Heavenly Stems and the last of the Heavenly Stems.

Nine at the top line: Doing divination under a bed, one's sacred ax is missing. Ill omen.

Notes:

1. 巽(xun): calculation. Some scholars have interpreted it as order, command; others as submission, obedience. According to the *I Ching on Silk* 巽(xun) is identical with 筭 which is an instrument for calculaton or divination. That is why in 象(xiang), one of the

125

Appedixes to I Ching, it says 巽，君子以申命行事(xun, jun zi yi shen ming xing shi)：Calculation：the superior man should take action in accordance with the lot known by divination.

2. 进退，利武人之贞(jin tui, li wu ren zhi zhen)：hesitation in advance or retreat. The military man should be steadfast and faithful. 武人(wu ren)：courageous military man.

3. 巽在床下，用史巫纷若(xun zai chuang xia, yong shi wu fen ruo)：the fortune-teller does divination under a bed. He also asks the officials of sacrifice and witches to help him with keeping disaters away. 史(shi)：an official in charge of offering sacrifice. 巫(wu)：witch. 纷若(fen ruo)：many.

4. 频巽(pin xun)：do divination frequently. 频(pin)is written as 编(bian) in the *I Ching on Silk*; a different interpretation is worry, distress.

5. 田获三品(tian huo san pin)：in hunting, one obtains game killed in three ways. 田(tian)：hunt. 三品(san pin)：animals killed in three different hunting ways. In ancient times the king or princes classified the game killed in hunting according to how they were killed. The first class is the game killed by being shot in the heart, which is used as sacrifice；the second is shot in the leg and used to entertain noble guests；the last is shot in the belly, which can be eaten by themselves. With respect to this expression, some scholars have advanced different interpretations：three kinds of animals such as wolf, swine and pheasant, or chicken, sheep and pheasant. These are not convincing interpretations.

6. 无初有终(wu shu you zhong)：not successful at first but a good result is attained on the last day. 初(chu)：the first of the ten Heavenly Stems, that is, 甲日(jia ri)：the first day. 终(zhong)：the last of the Heavenly Stems；i. e. 癸日(gui ri), the tenth day.

7. 先庚三日，后庚三日(xian geng san ri, hou geng san ri)：the days three days before or after 庚(geng), one of the ten Heavenly Stems.

According to the ten Heavenly Stems, the day of 丁(ding) and the day of 癸(gui) are respectively three days before or after the Heavenly Stem 庚(geng).

8. 丧其资斧 (sang qi zi fu): the sacred ax is missing. 资斧 (zi fu) is written as 濬斧 in the *I Ching on Silk*.

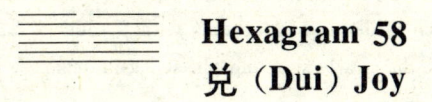

Hexagram 58
兑 (Dui) Joy

The Chinese text:

兑¹：亨，利贞。
初九：和兑²，吉。
九二：孚兑³，吉。悔亡。
六三：来兑⁴，凶。
九四：商兑未宁⁵，介疾有喜⁶。
九五：孚于剥⁷，有厉。
上六：引兑⁸。

Translation:

Joy: Great success. Advantageous to be steadfast and faithful.
Nine at the bottom line: It is auspicious if one has a pleasant and benign face.
Nine at the second line: It is favourable to be convinced with a pleasant and sincere mind. Regret vanishes.
Six at the third line: Misfortune arises if one looks for joy from flattery.
Nine at the fourth line: They discuss in a harmonious and pleasant way

but fail to reach an agreement. A slight ailment occurs but good luck will follow.

Nine at the fifth line: One enjoys stripping away. It is a peril.

Six at the top line: One is pleased with being introduced.

Notes:

1. 兑(dui): joy, happy. In the *I Ching on Silk* it is written as 夺(duo) which is identical in meaning with 兑(dui).

2. 和兑(he dui): a benign and pleasent countenance. 和(he): benign and harmonious.

3. 孚兑(fu dui): convinced with joy and sincerity in mind. 孚(fu): sincerity.

4. 来兑(lai dui): seek after joy from flattery.

5. 商兑未宁(shang dui wei ning): discuss in a calm and pleasant atmosphere but reach no conclusion. 商(shang): discuss. 宁(ning): calm, harmonious.

6. 介疾有喜(jie ji you xi): a slight ailment occurs but one will have good luck. 介疾(jie ji): slight illness.

7. 孚于剥(fu yu bao): enjoy stripping away. 剥(bao): peel off or strip away.

8. 引兑(yin dui): be happy with being introduced.

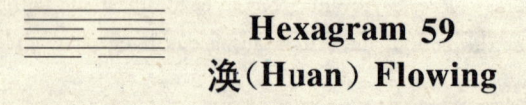

Hexagram 59
涣(Huan) Flowing

The Chinese text:

涣[1]: 亨, 王假有庙[2], 利涉大川, 利贞。

128

初六：用拯马壮³，吉。
九二：涣奔其机⁴，悔亡。
六三：涣其躬⁵，无悔。
六四：涣其群⁶，元吉。涣有丘⁷，匪夷所思⁸。
九五：涣汗其大号⁹，涣王居¹⁰。无咎。
上九：涣其血去，逖出¹¹，无咎。

Translation:

Dispersal: Great success. The king reaches a temple and makes an offering. It is advantageous to ford great rivers and practise the principle of faithfulness.

Six at the bottom line: To rescue with a strong horse. Auspicious.

Nine at the second line: The water flows to the stair steps of a building. Regrets disappear.

Six at the third line: No big trouble occurs although the water washes one's body.

Six at the fourth line: The water reaches a group of people. But it is not dangerous as expected because high land is found there.

Six at the fifth line: The command has been issued and cannot be taken back just as the water recedes. The water flows to the house of the king but no danger.

Nine at the top line: Fear and anxiety vanish as the water recedes. No disaster.

Notes:

1. 涣 (huan): flowing and receding of water. We adopt this interpretation from the previous scholars and according to the three *Appendixes to I Ching*, 杂卦 (za gua), 序卦 (xu gua) and 系辞 (xi ci). But we also doubt the absolute truth of this interpretation because when we review the context of this hexagram, we suspect that this

character means to call or shout in the ceremony of offering sacrifice.

2. 王假有庙 (wang jia you miao): the king arrives at a temple and offers sacrifice.

3. 用拯马壮 (yong zheng ma zhuang): to rescue with a strong horse. 拯 (zheng): rescue, save; it also means to take.

4. 涣奔其机 (huan ben qi ji): water flows to the stair step of the house. 机 (ji) is substituted by 阶 (jie) in the *I Ching on Silk*, according to which we interpret it as stairs steps of a building.

5. 涣其躬 (huan qi gong): water flows to and washes one's own body. 躬 (gong): one's own body.

6. 涣其群 (huan qi qun): water reaches a group of people. 群 (qun): a group of people, mass.

7. 涣有丘 (huan you qiu): water flows to the hillside. 丘 (qiu): hill, plateau.

8. 匪夷所思 (fei yi suo si): cannot think of it in a normal way. 匪 (fei): no, not. 夷 (yi): normal. usual.

9. 涣汗其大号 (huan han qi da hao): the issued command cannot be taken back as the water recedes. This interpretation is in accord with the foregoing lines and the *I Ching on Silk*. 号 (hao): issue an order loudly.

10. 涣王居 (huan wang ju): water laps at the king's mansion.

11. 涣其血去，逖出 (huan qi xue qu, ti chu): fear and anxiety vanish as the water recedes. 血 (xue) is identical with 恤 (xu), worry or anxiety. 逖 (ti) is rewritten as 汤 (tang) in the *I Ching on Silk*, meaning fear.

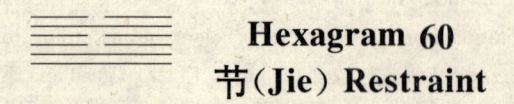

Hexagram 60
节 (Jie) Restraint

The Chinese text:

节¹：亨。苦节不可贞²。
初九：不出户庭³，无咎。
九二：不出门庭⁴，凶。
六三：不节若，则嗟若⁵，无咎。
六四：安节⁶，亨。
九五：甘节，吉，往有尚⁷。
上六：苦节，贞凶，悔亡。

Translation:

Restraint: Great success. The straws cannot be used in divination because their joints have withered.

Nine at the bottom line: No disaster occurs if one does not step out of the court-yard.

Nine at the second line: It brings misfortune if one does not step out of the front court-yard.

Six at the third line: Lavish spending will cause sighs and anxiety but not calamity.

Six at the fourth line: Be content with restraint. Great success.

Six at the fifth line: It is auspicious to enjoy thrift. One will be honoured with a reward if one goes there.

Six at the top line: It is misfortune to use the withered straw for divination. But regrets vanish.

Notes:

1. 节 (jie): restraint or thrift. This hexagram looks like a bamboo joint and also signifies the joint of a divination straw.
2. 苦节不可贞 (ku jie bu ke zhen): the straws cannot be used as the instrument of divination because their joints are withered. 苦 (ku) is

written as 枯 (ku) in the *I Ching on Silk* and means to wither. The accepted interpretation of the phrase " it is improper to be over-thrifty " is misleading.

3. 不出户庭 (bu chu hu ting): not step out of the court-yard. 户庭 (hu ting): court-yard.

4. 不出门庭 (bu chu men ting): not step out of the front court-yard. 门庭 (men ting): the outer court-yard within the front gate.

5. 不节若，则嗟若 (bu jie ruo, ze jie ruo): lavishness leads to worry and sighs. 嗟 (jie): to sigh.

6. 安节 (an jie): be satisfied with restraint.

7. 甘节，吉，往有尚 (gan jie, ji, wang you shang): favourable to enjoy frugality. A reward will be granted if one advances. 甘 (gan): sweet; its extended meaning is to enjoy or be content with. 尚 (shang): reward.

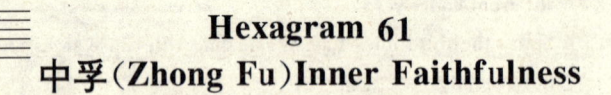

Hexagram 61
中孚 (Zhong Fu) Inner Faithfulness

The Chinese text:

中孚[1]: 豚鱼吉[2]。利涉大川。利贞。

初九: 虞吉，有它不燕[3]。

九地: 鸣鹤在阴，其子和之[4]。我有好爵，吾与尔靡之[5]。

六三: 得敌，或鼓或罢，或泣或歌[6]。

六四: 月几望，马匹亡[7]，无咎。

九五: 有孚挛如[8]，无咎。

上九: 翰音登于天[9]，贞凶。

Translation:

Inner Faithfulness: It is auspicious to offer a little pig and fish as sacrifice. Advantageous to cross the great rivers and remain faithful.
Nine at the first line: Having peace is good luck. Anxiety arises when an accident takes place.
Nine at the second line: A crane sings in the shade and the young ones follow it. I have good wine and will share it with you.
Six at the third line: Having defeated the enemy, some are beating drums, some are on the way back in triumph, some are weeping and some are singing.
Six at the fourth line: Horses will be missing on the sixteenth of the month but no disaster will happen.
Nine at the fifth line: Maintain love with sincerity and faithfulness. No trouble.
Nine at the top line: Offer sacrifice of a fowl to Heaven. Good omen.

Notes:

1. 中孚(zhong fu): faithfulness in one's heart. 孚(fu): faithful or sincere.

2. 豚鱼吉(tun yu ji): auspitious to offer a little pig and fish as sacrifice. 豚(tun): little pig.

3. 虞吉，有它不燕(yu ji, you ta bu yan): good fortune if one has peace. Anxiety arises if an accident happens. 虞(yu): peace. 它(ta): accident. 燕(yan) is written as 宁(ning) which is identical with 晏(yan), peace.

4. 鸣鹤在阴，其子和之(ming he zai yin, qi zi he zhi): a crane sings in the shade and the young ones follow it. 阴(yin): shade. 和(he): follow, accompany.

5. 我有好爵，吾与尔靡之(wo you hao jue, wu yu er mi zhi): I have

good wine and will share it with you. 好爵(hao jue): good wine. 爵(jue): wine cup; in this case it signifies wine. 尔(er): you. 靡(mi) is replaced by 纍(lei) in the *I Ching on Silk*. Both literally mean thick rope and by extension mean to share.

6. 得敌，或鼓或罢，或泣或歌(de di, huo gu huo ba, huo qi huo ge): having defeated the enemy, some beat drums, some return in triumph, some weep and some sing. 得(de): defeat. 或(huo): some people. 鼓(gu): beat drum. 罢(ba): (the army) return in triumph. 泣(qi): weep.

7. 月几望，马匹亡(yue ji wang, ma pi wang): horses are missing on the sixteenth day of the month.

8. 有孚挛如(you fu luan ru): to maintain love with sincerity and faithfulness(see the fifth line of Hexaram Xiao Xu).

9. 翰音登于天(han yin deng yu tian): worship Heaven with sacrifice of a fowl. 翰音(han yin): sacrificial fowl.

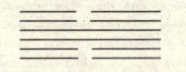

Hexagram 62
小过(Xiao Guo) Small Fault

The Chinese text:

小过[1]：亨，利贞。可小事，不可大事[2]。飞鸟遗之音[3]。不宜上，宜下[4]。大吉。

初六：飞鸟以凶[5]。

六二：过其祖，遇其妣[6]，不及其君，遇其臣[7]，无咎。

九三：弗过防之，从或戕之[8]，凶。

九四：无咎，弗过遇之，往厉必戒[9]，勿用，永贞[10]。

六五：密云不雨，自我西郊[11]，公弋取彼在穴[12]。

134

上六：弗遇过之，飞鸟离之[13]，凶，是谓灾眚。

Translation:

Small Fault: Great success. Advantageous to be steadily faithful. One can do small things but not the great ones. A bird's song is left when it has flown away. Inappropriate to go up but alright to do things while one is in a low position. Super fortune.

Six at the first line: A bird in flight gives rise to misfortune.

Six at the second line: Passing by the grandfather one sees one's grandmother. Without arriving at the king's place one meets with his ministers. No harm.

Nine at the third line: Guard against excesses lest you make a mistake. Indulgence leads to a danger of being slain. Ill omen.

Nine at the fourth line: It is harmless to encounter an error without making mistake. Dangerous if one goes forward, therefore one must be alert. Stop doing such things and always keep the principle of steadfast faithfulness.

Nine at the fifth line: A dense cloud arises in the western outskirts of our city but no rain falls. A prince shoots at a bird and then finds it in a cave.

Six at the top line: Meet with error without making mistake. A flying bird will be trapped in a net. Misfortune and a calamity indeed.

Notes:

1. 小过 (xiao guo): small fault. 过 (guo): experience or excess; its extended meaning is fault, sin.

2. 可小事，不可大事 (ke xiao shi, bu ke da shi): ordinary things can be done but not the great ones. 小事 (xiao shi): small or ordinary things. 大事 (da shi): important things such as military action and making sacrifice.

3. 飞鸟遗之音(fei niao yi zhi yin): the bird flys away but its song is left. 遗(yi): to be left.

4. 不宜上，宜下(bu yi shang, yi xia): advantageous to do things in a low rather than high position.

5. 飞鸟以凶(fei niao yi xiong): a flying bird brings bad luck. 以(yi): and, bring.

6. 过其祖，遇其妣(guo qi zu, yu qi bi): passing by one's grandfather to see one's grandmother. 祖(zu): grandfather. 妣(bi): grandmother, also a general name for mother.

7. 不及其君，遇其臣(bu ji qi jun, yu qi chen): before reaching the king's palace one encounters his ministers. 不及(bu ji): without or before reaching. 臣(chen): minister or servant; it is written as 仆(pu), servant.

8. 弗过防之，从或戕之(fu guo fang zhi, cong huo qiang zhi): guard against error in case one make a mistake. Indulgence results in the danger of being killed. 弗(fu): not, without. 从(cong) is synonymous with 纵(zong), indulgence. 或(huo): have, there is. 戕(qiang): kill, slay.

9. 弗过遇之，往厉必戒(fu guo yu zhi, wang li bi jie): meeting with fault without making mistakes. Any advance will encounter danger. Must be alert. 厉 (li): danger.

10. 勿用，永贞(wu yong, yong zhen): not do this matter and always keep the principle of steadfast faithfulness. 永 (yong): always, permanent. 贞(zhen): steadily faithful.

11. 密云不雨，自我西郊(mi yun bu yu, zi wo xi jiao): a dense cloud arises in the western outskirts of our city but no rain falls. (see Hexagram Xiao Xu).

12. 公弋取彼在穴(gong yi qu bi zai xue): having shot at a bird, the prince finds it in a cave. 弋(yi): an arrow with a rope which can be retrieved after shooting. It is written as 射(she) in the *I Ching on Silk*. 彼(bi): the bird shot by an arrow.

13. 弗遇过之，飞鸟离之 (fu yu guo zhi, fei niao li zhi)：meeting with fault without making mistake. A flying bird will be caught in a net. 离 (li)：the net to trap birds. It is written as 罗 (luo) in the *I Ching on Silk* which is identical with 离 in meaning.

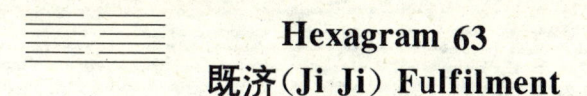

Hexagram 63
既济 (Ji Ji) Fulfilment

The Chinese text:

既济[1]：亨小，利贞[2]。初吉，终乱[3]。
初九：曳其轮，濡其尾[4]，无咎。
六二：妇丧其茀、勿逐[5]，七日得。
九三：高宗伐鬼方，三年克之[6]，小人勿用。
六四：繻有衣袽，终日戒[7]。
九五：东邻杀牛，不如西邻之禴祭[8]，实受其福[9]。
上六：濡其首[10]，厉。

Translation:

Fulfilment: One ought to be steadily faithful when one succeeds a little. Good fortune at the beginning but disorder in the end.
Nine at the bottom line: (Fording a river) one drags the wheel of a carriage and its rear part gets wet.
Six at the second line: A lady loses her hair ornament. Do not seek it and it will be found in seven days.
Nine at the third line: It took King Gao Zong three years to conquer the devil's land. Do not promote the lesser man.
Six at the fourth line: (A boat is) leaking and getting wet, one plugs

the leak with clothes. Be cautious all day long.

Nine at the fifth line: The neighbour to the east offers lavish sacrifices with a slaughtered ox. The neighbour to the west offers a simple sacrifice. But the former is less benefited and blessed by Heaven than the latter.

Six at the top line: One's head gets wet. It shows danger.

Notes:

1. 既济 (ji ji): fulfilment, after acomplishment. 既 (ji): already, after. 济 (ji): fulfilment, success. Its original meaning is to ford a river.

2. 亨小, 利贞 (heng xiao, li zhen): remain faithful when one has succeeded a little. 亨小 (heng xiao): little success.

3. 初吉, 终乱 (chu ji, zhong luan): good fortune at the beginning but disorder in the end.

4. 曳其轮, 濡其尾 (ye qi lun, ru qi wei): the wheel being dragged, the cart end gets wet. 曳 (ye): draw, drag. 轮 (lun): cart wheel. It is written as 纶 (lun) in the *I Ching on Silk*. 濡 (ru): get wet.

5. 妇丧其茀、勿逐 (fu sang qi fu, wu zhu): A lady loses her hair ornament; do not look for it. 茀 (fu) is identical to 髯、髶 and in the *I Ching on Silk* it is written as 发 (fa); here it refers to an ornament in general.

6. 高宗伐鬼方, 三年克之 (gao zong fa gui fang, san nian ke zhi): King Gao Zong warred against the devil's land. He subdued it in three years. 高宗 (gao zong): a well-known king named Wu Ding in the period of Yin, the Shang Dynasty. 鬼方 (gui fang): the devil's land, referring to a country near the north-west frontier of Shang. According to recently unearthed documents, King Gao Zong warred with the two countries 苦方 (ku fang) and 土方 (tu fang); It is also said that Tu Fang is Gui Fang and also that Gui Fang is Mongolia.

7. 繻有衣袽, 终日戒 (ru you yi ru, zhong ri jie): a boat leaks and one

stops the leak with clothes. Be cautious all day long. 繻 (ru) is identical to 襦 (ru) and 濡 (ru); meaning get wet. 袽 (ru): old clothes.

8. 东邻杀牛,不如西邻之礿祭(dong lin sha niu, bu ru xi lin zhi yue ji): the neighbour to the east which slaughters an ox as a lavish sacrifice is not so benefited as the neighbour to the west which offers a simple sacrifice. 东邻(dong lin): the neighbour to the east; someone interpreted it as the people in Shang. 西邻(xi lin): the neighbour to the west, the people in Zhou. 礿 (yue): the Spring or Summer sacrifices offered respectively by Shang and Zhou.

9. 实受其福(shi shou qi fu): be benefitted and blessed by Heaven. 受 (shou): receive benefit.

10. 濡其首(ru qi shou): one's head gets wet (when fording a river).

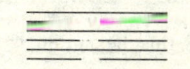

Hexagram 64
未济（Wei Ji）Unfulfilment

The Chinese text:

未济¹：亨。小狐汔济,濡其尾²,无攸利。
初六：濡其尾,吝。
九二：曳其轮,贞吉³。
六三：未济,征凶,利涉大川。
九四：贞吉,悔亡。震用伐鬼方⁴,三年有赏于大国⁵。
六五：贞吉,无悔,君子之光有孚⁶,吉。
上九：有孚于饮酒⁷,无咎。濡其首,有孚失是⁸。

Translation:

Unfaithfulness; Great success. A fox's tail gets wet when it has nearly

139

crossed a river. It is unfavourable.

Six at the bottom line: The wet tail indicates a future disgrace.

Nine at the second line: The cart wheel is dragged. Good omen.

Six at the third line: No success. It is misfortune to take military action but advantageous to ford great rivers.

Nine at the fourth line: Good omen and regret vanishes. The people of Zhou warred against the devil's land and conquered it in three years. They are granted a reward in the great country.

Six at the fifth line: Good fortune and no regret. It is appropriate that the glory of the superior man consists in his sincerity and faithfulness.

Nine at the top line: It is harmless that one shows sincerity and faithfulness in drinking wine. Sincere but incorrect if one is so drunk as to get one's head wet.

Notes:

1. 未济 (wei ji): Unfulfilment. The name of this hexagram is in contrast to the preceding one.

2. 小狐汔济,濡其尾 (xiao hu qi ji, ru qi wei): having nearly crossed a river, the fox gets its tail wet. 汔 (qi): nearly, almost. It is written as 气 (qi) in the *I Ching on Silk*. 濡 (ru): gets wet.

3. 曳其轮,贞吉 (ye qi lun, zhen ji): dragging the cart wheel indicates good fortune. 曳 (ye): drag, draw.

4. 震用伐鬼方 (zhen yong fa gui fang): mobilise an army to fight against the devil's land. Here it means that Zhou waged a war against the devil's land. 震 (zhen): tremble, mobilise.

5. 三年有赏于大国 (san nian you shang yu da guo): (the people) defeat the enemy in three years and are rewarded in the great country. 赏 (shang): reward. 于 (yu): in, at. 大国 (da guo): great country; denoting the state of Shang here.

6. 君子之光有孚 (jun zi zhi guang you fu): the glory of the superior man consists in his sincerity and faithfulness. 光 (guang): glory,

honour. 孚(fu): faithfulness.

7. 有孚于饮酒(you fu yu yin jiu): sincerity and faithfulness can be found in drinking wine.

8. 有孚失是(you fu shi shi): sincere but incorrect. 失是(shi shi): incorrect.

鲁新登字 12 号

周易古经白话解

刘大钧　林忠军　著
傅有德　　　　译
弗兰克·劳伦　审校

*

中国山东友谊出版社出版
（中国山东济南胜利大街 39 号）
中国山东人民印刷厂印刷
中国国际图书贸易总公司发行
（中国北京车公庄西路 35 号）
北京邮政信箱第 399 号　邮政编码 100044
版次：（英文版）
1995 年 2 月第 1 版　1995 年 2 月第 1 次印刷
ISBN7—80551—696—0/B·5
02500
17—E—2928P